W9-APG-941

ENGLISH GRAMMAR SIMPLIFIED

ENGLISH GRAMMAR SIMPLIFIED

Blanche Ellsworth
John A. Higgins

HarperCollins*College*Publishers

Sponsoring Editor: Jane Kinney
Developmental Editor: Leslie Taggart
Project Coordination: Americomp
Cover Design: Theresa Delgado
Production Manager: Michael Weinstein
Compositor: Americomp
Printer and Binder: R R Donnelley & Sons, Company
Cover Printer: The Lehigh Press, Inc.

English Grammar Simplified, Sixth Edition
Copyright © 1992 by HarperCollins Publishers, Inc.

All rights reserved. Printed in the United States of America. No part of this book may be used or reproduced in any manner whatsoever without written permission, except in the case of brief quotations embodied in critical articles and reviews. For information address HarperCollins College Publishers, 10 East 53d Street, New York, NY 10022.

Library of Congress Cataloging-in-Publication Data
ISBN 0-06-501148-1
92 93 94 95   9 8 7 6 5 4 3 2 1

CONTENTS

PREFACE

English Grammar Simplified is a complete reference guide for writing. Sections on grammar, punctuation, mechanics, and usage make this a comprehensive guide to writing correct and effective sentences and making appropriate word choices. A section on spelling offers both a list of commonly misspelled words and a selection of proven techniques for spelling improvement. "Beyond the Sentence" puts sentence writing into the larger context of paragraphs and also shows methods for outlining ideas before writing. "Documentation" serves as a concise reference to three widely used styles of documenting sources in research writing: MLA, APA, and Chicago.

The structure of *English Grammar Simplified* makes it extremely easy to use. The outline format, extensive cross-referencing, and comprehensive index make finding solutions to writing problems simple.

Concise explanations, an abundance of examples, and comprehensive coverage make *English Grammar Simplified* an easy-to-use guide to writing clearly and effectively.

ENGLISH GRAMMAR SIMPLIFIED

He has washed my wool sweaters in the washing machine, which can now fit neither of us.

People who are taking the bus are complaining because they are not working the way they are supposed to.

We ate all the oysters it made him and I feel badly.

Well-intentioned adults wrote the preceding sentences, thinking them clear and correct. Without an understanding of the basic grammar of the English sentence, we can easily fall into such pitfalls of language. This section of *English Grammar Simplified* explains basic grammar concisely, in the most common terms, to help you create sentences that are clear, correct, and effective.

G-1.   The Sentence and Its Parts

A sentence is a grammatically independent unit of expression, made up of two essential parts called the **subject** and the **predicate**. In writing, a sentence begins with a capital letter and ends with a period, question mark, or exclamation point.

1. The Two Main Parts of a Sentence

A. The Subject. The **subject** of a sentence (the **complete subject**) is the part naming the person or thing that the sentence speaks about. That person or thing itself is called the **simple subject** (or just **subject**):

> [complete subject in *italics;* simple subject in **bold print**]

*The old **road** along the coast* leads you to the bridge.
*A noted **scientist** from France* will speak here tonight.
*Poor old **Dr. Faust*** is finally retiring from the college.

B. The Predicate. The **predicate** of a sentence (**complete predicate**) is the part that speaks about the subject. It tells what the subject *does* or asserts that the subject *is* something.

(1) *The simple predicate:* The key word (or words) in the predicate— the word stating the actual doing or being—is called the **simple predicate** (or just **predicate**) or **verb:**

> [complete predicate in *italics*; simple predicate in **bold**]

The old road along the coast ***leads*** *you to the bridge.*
A noted scientist from France ***will speak*** *here tonight.*
Poor old Dr. Faust ***is*** *finally **retiring*** *from the college.*

(2) *Complements*: A **complement** is a word needed to complete the meaning of some verbs: Sandra saw *Orson*. Lincoln was a *Republican*. See G-3.2B, page 7.

NOTE: A subject, predicate (verb), or complement may be **compound**; that is, it may have two or more parts joined by *and*, *or*, or *but*.

[compound subject and complement in *italics;* compound predicate in **bold**]

Joey or Martha will get the tickets.
The waiter **tripped and fell** over the diner's legs.
Poems and stories **delight and edify** *children, teenagers, and adults.*

2. The Sentence Pattern. Subject, Verb, and Complement(s)

usually occur in a standard order, or pattern: **S V (C) (C)**. This means that the subject [**S**] comes first, then the verb [**V**], then—perhaps—one or two complements [**(C)**]. This normal order is altered in most interrogative and exclamatory sentences (see 3 below). Other sentences can alter the normal order:

    V   **S**
Here are the books.

     V S V   **C**
Never have I seen such chaos.

Sentences beginning with expletives (*there*, *it*) reverse the normal subject–verb order (see G-9.1I, page 31):

    V   **S**
There is a dress that will fit you.

3. Ways of Classifying Sentences
A. By Purpose

Declarative (a statement): You are my friend.
Interrogative (a question): Are you my friend?
Imperative (a command or request): Close the door.
Exclamatory (an expression of emotion): How glad I am!

B. By Structure, according to the number and kinds of clauses they

contain. A sentence may be **simple, compound, complex,** or **compound-complex.** G-8.3, page 27, explains these categories in detail.

G-2.   The Parts of Speech: A Survey

Every word performs one of five functions: *naming, expressing doing or being, modifying, connecting,* or *expressing emotion.* In traditional grammar, these functions are classified into eight **parts of speech:** *noun, pronoun,* *verb, adjective, adverb, preposition, conjunction,* and *interjection.* Learning to recognize the parts of speech will help you write with greater ease, confidence, and accuracy.

1. Words That Name

A. Nouns: A noun is a word that names a person, place, or thing (including a quality or idea):

Person: Maria, woman, Millard Fillmore, doctor
Place: Chicago, Yellowstone Park, waterfront, earth
Thing: shoe, car, dog, carrot, Statue of Liberty, love, strength, courage, democracy, height

See G-3, page 7, for details about nouns.

B. Pronouns (*pro-* means "for" or "instead of"): As its name suggests, a pronoun takes the place of (stands for) a noun. The noun that a pronoun stands for is called the **antecedent** of that pronoun:

[pronoun in **bold**; antecedent in *italics*]

Sally took three suitcases with **her** to Paris.
When the *Martians* come, **they** may not harm Earth at all.
Although *Ms. Brown* has arrived, **she** hasn't checked into **her** hotel yet.

See G-6, page 18, for details about pronouns.

2. Words That Express Doing or Being: Verbs.

A verb asserts something about the subject of a sentence. It tells what the subject *does, did, or will do* (an **action verb**) or tells that the subject *is, was, or will be* something (a **linking verb**):

Action: The arrow *pierced* the target. [tells what the subject, *arrow,* did]
Linking: The arrow *is* an accurate weapon. [tells that the subject is something]

Some verbs consist of several words: a main **verb** preceded by one or more **auxiliary** (helping) **verbs:**

[main verb in **bold**; auxiliary verbs in *italics*]

Aloysius *had* **sought** Fayella in vain.
She *might have been* **thrown** into the river.
You *did* **say** you were sorry, didn't you?

The verb in a sentence is also called the (**simple**) **predicate.** See G-4, page 9, for details about verbs.

3. Words that Modify.

To *modify* means "to change." A word that modifies changes or clarifies our concept of another word.

A. Adjectives: An adjective modifies a noun (or occasionally a pronoun). It describes that noun or limits its meaning. **Descriptive adjectives** tell *what kind: small* car (what kind of car?), *green* rug, *unimaginable* brutality, *odoriferous ten-cent* cigar. **Limiting adjectives (determiners)** tell *which one* or *how many*. There are several kinds of limiting adjectives:

Possessive: *my* auto, *her* grades, *their* policy [which auto, grades, policy?]
Demonstrative: *this* auto, *those* grades, *that* policy
Indefinite: *any* auto, *either* grade, *many* policies
Interrogative: *which* auto? *whose* grades? *what* policy?
Numerical: *one* auto, *two* grades, *third* policy
Articles: *an* auto, *the* grades, *a* policy

As these examples show, an adjective usually appears directly before the noun it modifies. A descriptive adjective can appear also after a linking verb (as a complement). Such an adjective describes the subject to which the verb links it:

    S   V   C
My car is *small*. [*Small* describes the subject, *car*.]
Our bedroom rug looks *green*.
The problem remains *serious*.

B. **Adverbs:** An adverb usually modifies a verb. It describes *how, when, where, or to what degree* the action of a verb is done. There are several kinds of adverbs:

Manner: Brenda drives *carefully*. [drives how?]
Time: Brenda drove *yesterday*. [drove when?]
Place: Brenda drove *everywhere*. [drove where?]
Degree: Brenda studies *enough*. [studies to what degree?]

An adverb phrase or clause can also describe *why*.
    Some adverbs can modify an adjective or another adverb. Such adverbs are called **adverbs of degree** (or **intensifiers**):

Brenda drives *quite* carefully. [carefully to what degree? how carefully?] She prefers *very* cautious behavior.

That report was the *least* helpful she had ever read. [helpful to what degree? how helpful?]

For **conjunctive adverbs,** see P-5B, page 47.

4. Words That Connect
A. **Conjunctions:** A conjunction joins other words or word groups. There are two kinds of conjunctions:

(1) *A coordinate conjunction (and, but, or, nor, for, yet, so)* joins words or word groups of the same kind and same importance:

Words: Jack *and* Jill
        small *yet* fierce
        speaking *or* listening
Word groups (phrases): up the hill *and* into the woods
    to jump easily *but* not to fall gracefully
    hoping to win *yet* feeling unsure

Word groups (clauses): Jack fell down, *and* Jill came tumbling after.

Jeff smiled, *for* he enjoyed the show.

He will laugh, *or* he will cry.

NOTE: And, but, or, or *nor* may be used with other words to form a **correlative conjunction:** *not only . . . but also,* (*n*)*either . . .* (*n*)*or, both . . . and:*

Both Jack *and* Jill went up the hill.

Neither Jack *nor* Jill enjoyed the outing.

She had trained *not only* as a lawyer *but also* as a doctor.

See U, page 88, on using *so.*

(2) *A subordinate conjunction* (*if, because, although, when, unless,* etc.) joins a dependent (subordinate) clause to an independent (main) clause. The subordinate conjunction begins the dependent clause: *if you love me;* **because** *they were late:*

If you love me, you will never release that letter.

You will never release that letter *if you love me.*

They ate in a hurry *because they were late.*

Because they were late, they ate in a hurry.

Do not write a subordinate clause alone as if it were a sentence.

Wrong: You will never release that letter. If you love me.

G-10.2A, page 34, discusses this error (a *fragment*).

Other common subordinate conjunctions:

whenever	while	as
since	before	after
until	as soon as	so that
in order that	(even) though	whereas
whether	where	wherever
as if	as though	than
provided	except that	in case

NOTE: Other kinds of words that join clauses are **relative pronouns** (such as *who* or *which*—see G-8.2A, C, page 26) and **conjunctive adverbs** (such as *therefore* or *however*—see P-5B, page 47).

Coordinate conjunctions are sometimes called **coordinators** and subordinate conjunctions **subordinators.**

B. **Prepositions:** A preposition is a connecting word such as *in, on, of, for,* or *into* that shows how a noun is related to the sentence containing it:

The bird flew *into* the cage.

The bird flew *over* the cage.

The bird flew *around* the cage.

Each preposition above shows a different relation between the noun *cage* and the action of the sentence.

Other common prepositions:

to	toward	from
above	under	beneath
underneath	below	past
by	onto	upon
behind	beside	through
out (of)	off	between
among	near	next to
in front of	against	about
within	inside	outside
at	up	down
before	during	until
since	besides	except
like	despite	instead of
because of	in addition to	as well as

The word group beginning with the preposition and ending with the noun is called a **prepositional phrase.** The noun (or pronoun) is called the **object of the preposition:**

[preposition in **bold;** object of preposition in *italics*]

with all her *friends*
of the *night*
for *me*

5. Words That Express Emotion: Interjections. Unlike the other kinds of words, the interjection has little or no grammatical connection with the rest of a sentence:

Mild interjection (punctuated with comma): *Well,* I wouldn't worry about that.
Strong interjection (punctuated with exclamation point): *No!* I can't believe it.

6. The Same Word as Different Parts of Speech. The way a word is used in a particular sentence determines its part of speech in that sentence. To determine the part of speech of a word in a particular appearance in a sentence, examine its grammatical use (**syntax**) in that sentence: if it names something, it is a noun; if it describes a noun, it is an adjective; and so forth:

Noun: Turn on the *light.*
Adjective: I prefer *light* colors in my room.
Verb: Why didn't you *light* a fire?

You can often determine a word's part of speech by its position or its ending. For example, a word following a limiting adjective (*a, my, this,* etc.) is likely to be a noun: *my* **brother**, *this* **test,** *any* **person**. (Another adjective may intervene: *this* impossible **test**).

A word following an auxiliary verb is likely to be a verb: *has* **grown**, *might have been* **saved**, *should* **know**. (An adverb may come between the auxiliary and the main verb: *has* hardly **grown**).

Most words with an *-ly* ending are adverbs: *slowly, awkwardly, quietly.*

Words ending in *-tion, -ity, -ness,* or *-ment* are usually nouns: *perfection, purity, fineness, contentment.*

Words ending in *-ify* or *-ize* are probably verbs: *calcify, winterize.*

Words ending in -al, -ous, -ful, or *-less* are probably adjectives: *vernal, ridiculous, wonderful, careless.*

G-3. Using Nouns

Recall that nouns name persons, places, or things.

1. Kinds of Nouns. Nouns are classified in several ways:

    A. Singular or Plural: A **singular** noun names one person, thing, etc.: *house, chair, woman, city.* A **plural** noun names two or more persons, things, etc.: *houses, chairs, women, cities.* Most singular nouns become plural by the addition of *-s.* See S-1.6E, page 70, for rules on the formation of plurals.

    B. Common or Proper: A **common** noun names one or more members of a class of things: *woman, women, chair, auditorium, mice, city.* A **proper** noun names a specific person, place, or thing: *Joan Shea, Carnegie Hall, Mickey Mouse, Kansas City.*

    C. Concrete or Abstract: A **concrete** noun names an object that can be perceived by the senses: *woman, Joan Shea, mice, cheese.* An **abstract** noun names a quality or idea: *liberty, sadness, ambition, love, tragedy, height.*

    D. Collective: A **collective** noun names a group of persons or things: *jury, team, flock, committee, army, class, band.*

2. The Five Main Uses of Nouns. Recall the basic sentence pattern: S V (C) (C). That is, each sentence has a subject, a verb, and possibly one or two complements. The subject and the complements are usually nouns.

    A. Subject of a Sentence. The **subject** tells *who or what* if placed before the verb:

    Pattern: **S** V (C) (C).

    Fred smokes. [Who smokes?]
    The *trains* were late. [What were late?]

Sarah and *Ivan* are planning a European vacation. [Who are planning? (compound subject)]

B. Complement. A **complement** is a word in the predicate that completes the meaning of the verb. There are four kinds of complements:

(1) *A direct object* is a noun (or pronoun) that tells *whom or what* after an action verb.

Pattern: S V **C**

I opened the *package*. [opened what?]
The city is employing *teenagers*. [employing whom?]
The fans cheered the *players* and the *coach*. [compound complement]

(2) *An indirect object* is a noun (or pronoun) that appears after certain action verbs, telling *to* or *for whom*, or *to* or *for what*, the action of the verb is done.

Pattern: S V **C** (indirect object) C (direct object)

Flo sent *Tony* a present. [sent to whom?]
Tony had done *Flo* a favor. [done for whom?]
Marcia bought *Tony* and *Flo* a new dog. [compound indirect object]

(3) *A subjective complement* (predicate nominative) is a noun (or pronoun) that follows a linking verb and renames or explains the subject.

Pattern: S V (linking) **C**

Henfield was the Democratic *candidate*. [*Candidate* gives another name or title for *Henfield*.]
A kumquat is a *fruit*. [*Fruit* explains what *kumquat* is.]

NOTE: An adjective can also be a subjective complement:

Henfield is *unbeatable*.
The tree seems *dead*.

For a full list of linking verbs, see G-4.2C, page 10.

(4) *An objective complement* is a noun that follows a direct object and renames or explains it.

Pattern: S V C (direct object) **C** (objective complement)

They called Henfield a *hero*. [*Hero* gives another name or title for *Henfield*.]
The electors declared Henfield the *winner*.
Their angry parents considered Sheila and Bob the biggest *culprits*.

The objective complement occurs most commonly with such verbs as *call, name, elect, designate, consider, appoint*, and *think*.

NOTE: An adjective can also be an objective complement:

They called Henfield *heroic.*
She finds Jack *handsome.*

C. An Object of a Preposition is a noun (or pronoun) that ends a prepositional phrase and answers the question *whom* or *what* after the preposition:

Jeanne lives near *Frieda.* [near whom?]
Smyth did her duty with supreme *courage.* [with what?]
Her parents are optimistic about her *future.* [about what?]

D. An Appositive is a noun that follows and renames or further identifies another noun:

Henfield, the incumbent *senator,* has been reelected.
That man insulted Prince Karl, the queen's *nephew.*
They bought an expensive toy, a handmade wooden *doll.*

E. Direct Address. A noun (or pronoun) in **direct address** names the person being spoken to:

Noun: *Marie,* you've won the lottery!
Pronoun: Get over here, *you!*

G-4.   Using Verbs

A verb is the core of every sentence. Without a verb, a group of words is only a fragment of a sentence instead of a complete sentence. Even if a sentence contains only one word, that word must be a verb: *Run! Wait.* (Every verb must have a subject, expressed or understood. In sentences such as *Run!* and *Wait,* the subject is understood to be *you.*) The function of a verb is to assert something about its subject—that is, to tell what the subject *does* (*did, will do*) or that the subject *is* (*was, will be*) something:

Birds *sing.*
The flowers *were blooming* everywhere.
Marie *is* this year's valedictorian.
Thomas *will graduate* in June.

1. Identifying the Verb. There is a simple way to identify the verb in a sentence. The verb is the word that will usually change its form if you change the time of the sentence:

Nowadays I *work* in Canarsie.
Long ago I *worked* in Canarsie.
For years I *have worked* in Canarsie.
Next spring I *will work* in Canarsie.

2. Kinds of Verbs. A verb is classified according to the kind of complement (if any) that follows it. In addition, there is a special kind of verb called an **auxiliary** (or **helping**) verb that may accompany a main verb.

A. **A Transitive Verb** is one that needs a direct object to complete its meaning. That is, it expresses an action that passes across (transits) from a doer—the subject—to a receiver—the direct object:

> The batter *hit* the ball. [*Batter* did the action, hitting; *ball* (direct object) received the action.]
> The judge *explained* the rules. [*Judge* did the action; *rules* received the action.]
> The letter carrier *opened* the mailbox. [*Letter carrier* did the action; *mailbox* received the action.]

B. **An Intransitive Verb** is one that does not need a direct object to complete its meaning. It expresses an action that does not have a receiver:

> Sally *sneezed.*
> Lincoln *died* in 1865. [*In 1865* = prepositional phrase, not direct object.]
> Portnoy *obeyed* promptly. [*Promptly* = adverb, not direct object.]

NOTE: Many verbs can be transitive in some uses and intransitive in others:

> He *begins* his speech with a joke. [*Begins* is transitive; *speech* is the direct object.]
> Work on the farm *begins* at sunrise. [*Begins* is intransitive; *at sunrise* is a preprositional phrase.]

> The boy *blows* bubbles. [Transitive]
> The wind *blows.* [Intransitive]

> Portnoy *obeyed* his master. [Transitive]
> Portnoy *obeyed* promptly. [Intransitive]

Dictionaries label each meaning of a verb as *v.t.* (*verb, transitive*) or *v.i.* (*verb, intransitive*).

C. **A Linking (State-of-Being, Copulative) Verb** expresses no action at all. It merely expresses state of being; it indicates a link of identity or description between the subject and the subjective complement following the verb:

> Foster *is* the vice-president. [*Foster* = *vice-president.*]
> This train *has been* late all week. [*Late* describes *train.*]
> Jack *became* a grouch. [*Jack* = *grouch.*]

The chief linking verb is *be*. Its parts include *am, is, are, was, were, being, been.* Other linking verbs are *become; seem;* any that mean roughly the same as *be, become,* or *seem,* such as *appear, grow, turn, remain, prove;* and the verbs of the five senses—*look, sound, feel, smell, taste.* Some verbs may be linking verbs in one sense and action verbs in another:

Linking	Action
I *looked* disheveled.	I *looked* out the window.
Nancy *grew* pensive.	Nancy *grew* cabbages.
Joe *turned* red.	Joe *turned* up the soil.

D. Auxiliary (Helping) Verbs. A verb may contain more than one word, as in *could have helped.* The last word in the verb is the **main verb**. The others are called auxiliary verbs, or simply **auxiliaries**. They convey some condition of the main verb, such as tense or mood. Only a few verbs can be auxiliaries:

have	be (am, is . . .)	do
will	would	shall
should	can	could
may	might	must
have to	ought (to)	need (to)
dare (to)		

The plane **had** *left* Hawaii.
The plane **is** *flying* here nonstop.
The plane **will be** *landing* soon.
The plane **did** *arrive* on time.
The plane **should** *arrive* on time.
The plane **must** certainly **have** *landed* by now. [Note that other words may come between parts of the verb.]
Would neither of you **have** *offered* assistance?

NOTE: Verbs of more than one word are sometimes called **verb phrases**. Auxiliaries such as *would, should*, and *can* are sometimes called **modals**.

3. Correct, Effective Use of Verbs

A. Know the Principal Parts of the Verb. The **principal parts** are the parts you need to know to form all six tenses. They are

	Regular Verb	Irregular Verb
Present Tense:	play	see
Past Tense:	played	saw
Past Participle:	played	seen

Regular verbs form their past tense and past participle by adding *-ed* to the present (with some minor spelling changes, as in *stopped, cried*). Irregular verbs form these parts in various ways. Some change vowels within the verb: *swim, swam, swum*. Some change a consonant: *build, built, built*. Some do not change: *cost, cost, cost*. Some change and add an ending: *break, broke, broken*. Consult your dictionary when in doubt about verb forms, for you cannot safely take one irregular verb as a model for another; consider *make* and *take*. See G-4D on page 13.

Some texts and dictionaries give a fourth principal part, the **present participle** (formed by adding *-ing* to the present form: *seeing, playing*). It is always regular, except for some minor spelling changes (as in *stopping, loving*).

B. **Use the Correct Tense of a Verb.** Verbs change form to show the time of the action or linking that they express. There are six tenses.

(1) The *present tense* expresses action or linking occurring now, regularly, or always:

I *see* him.
Walter *takes* the 8:02 daily.
Water *freezes* at 0° Celsius.
The sky *is* blue.

It can also indicate future action:

The bus *leaves* in an hour.

Two alternate forms of the present are the **progressive**, formed with *be* and the present participle (*-ing* form) of the main verb, and the **emphatic**, formed with *do* or *does* and the main verb:

Walter *is taking* the 8:02 today. [progressive]
Water *does freeze* at 0° Celsius. [emphatic]

(2) The *past tense* expresses action or linking completed at a specific time in the past:

I *saw* him.
Walter *took* the 8:02 yesterday.
She *was* sorry.

The progressive uses *was* or *were* and the *-ing* form. The emphatic uses *did*:

Walter *was taking* the 8:02 to work. [progressive]
The water *did freeze* even though you said it wouldn't. [emphatic]

(3) The *future tense* expresses action or linking that will take place in the future:

I *will see* him.
Walter *will take* the 8:02 tomorrow.
She *will be* sorry.

The progressive uses *will be* and the *-ing* form (there is no future emphatic):

Walter *will be taking* the 8:02 tomorrow.
I *will be seeing* him next week.

NOTE: In the future and future perfect tenses, many careful writers still prefer to use *shall* instead of *will* after *I* and *we:* I *shall return*. We *shall have left* by then.

(4) The *present perfect* tense expresses action or linking in which the past is connected to the present (*perfect* in this sense means "completed"):

She *has lived* here for forty years. [She still lives here.]

I *have seen* her twice this week. [Implying that the act of seeing her, or its effects, is continuing into the present]

Now we *have completed* our work. [We completed it at the present time.]

The progressive uses *have been* or *has been* and the *-ing* form (there is no emphatic form in the perfect tenses):

She *has been living* here forty years.

I *have been seeing* her every day for the last month.

(5) The *past perfect* tense expresses the earlier of two completed actions or linkings:

I said [yesterday] that I *had seen* her [last week].

We *had* already *left* town before we remembered that we had to go to the bank.

Until their credit card bills came, they *had*n't *thought* of all the consequences of quitting their jobs.

The progressive uses *had been* and the *-ing* form:

I *had been seeing* her.

She *had been thinking* that she ought to find another job.

(6) The *future perfect* tense expresses action or linking to be completed before a given future time:

She *will have seen* him by Sunday.

The baby *will have been* to the doctor twice by the time he is two months old.

The progressive uses *will have been* and the *-ing* form:

She *will have been seeing* him for a year on Friday.

We *will have been dancing* for twenty-four hours at midnight.

C. Use a Verb That Agrees in Person and Number with Its Subject. G-9, page 28, deals with the very important topic of agreement. See G-9.1A, page 28, for an explanation of person.

D. Distinguish a Verbal from a Verb. A **verbal** is a form derived from a verb. It is used not as a verb but as a noun, adjective, or adverb. There are three kinds of verbals: **infinitives, participles,** and **gerunds.**

(1) *Infinitive (to + verb),* used as
- Noun: *To worry* is futile. [subject]
  - Toni wants *to travel.* [direct object]
  - Toni's ambition is *to travel.* [subjective complement]
- Adjective: This is the road *to take.* [modifies *road*]
- Adverb: This book is easy *to read.* [modifies *easy*]
  - She came *to help.* [modifies *came*]

(2) *Participle,* used as adjective:
- Present participle (verb + *-ing*):

The *burning* house began to collapse. [modifies *house*]
The house, *burning* furiously, began to collapse. [modifies *house*]

• Past participle (third principal part of verb: for regular verbs, verb + *-ed;* for irregular verbs, no set form but often ends in *-en*):

The *burned* child was given first aid. [modifies *child*]
Badly *burned,* the child was given first aid. [modifies *child*]
The papers, *forgotten* in her haste, lay on her desk.

(3) *Gerund* (verb + *-ing*), used as noun:

Seeing is *believing.* [subject, subjective complement]
They condone *surviving* by *stealing.* [direct object, object of preposition]

See also G-6.2D(2), page 22; P-6.1A(3), page 48.

NOTE: An *-ing* verbal may be either a gerund or a participle, depending on its use in a particular sentence:

Swimming is excellent exercise. [gerund used as subject noun]
The *swimming* child reached the raft. [participle used as adjective, modifying *child*]

Matt enjoys *running.* [gerund: used as direct object]
Gerald watched the *running* horse, wishing he had bet on it. [participle: used as adjective, modifying *horse.*]

4. Avoid These Errors in Verb Use.

A. Do Not Shift Tense Without Reason.

Wrong: In chapter 1, Nick *moved* to Long Island and *rents* a house.
Right: In chapter 1, Nick *moved* to Long Island and *rented* a house.
Right: In chapter 1, Nick *moves* to Long Island and *rents* a house.

B. Avoid Needless Use of the Passive Voice. Transitive verbs have two voices. In the **active voice,** the more common one, the subject is the doer of the verb's action:

A million citizens rousingly *cheered* the queen.
An accountant *prepares* my tax return.

In the **passive voice,** the receiver of the action becomes the subject, and the doer (if mentioned at all) appears in a *by* phrase:

The queen *was cheered* rousingly by a million citizens.
My tax return *is prepared* by an accountant.

The passive voice is formed from the past participle of the verb, preceded by the appropriate form of *be: am cheered, was taken, might have been told, will be shot.* In general, the active voice, which stresses the doer of an action, is more forceful than the passive, which stresses the receiver:

Stronger: With great difficulty we *reached* the summit.
Weaker: With great difficulty the summit *was reached* by us.

But when the doer of the action is unknown, unimportant, or to be deemphasized, the passive is appropriate:

My apartment *was broken* into last night.
Dinner *is served.*
Yes, an error *has been made* in this office.

C. **Do Not Shift Mood Without Reason.** The mood of a verb indicates how the idea of a sentence is to be regarded. Sentences that state facts or ask questions are in the **indicative mood:**

There *are* five horses in the corral.
How many horses *are* there in the corral?

Requests and commands are in the **imperative mood:**

Count the horses in the corral. [*You* is understood as the subject.]

The **subjunctive mood** expresses doubt, uncertainty, wish, or supposition or signals a condition contrary to fact. In the subjunctive mood, *am, is,* and *are* become *be; was* becomes *were; has* becomes *have;* and -*s* endings are dropped from other verbs:

Wish: God *be* with you. Long *live* the queen.
Doubt or uncertainty: If he *were* able to do it, it would take a long time.
Condition contrary to fact: If I *were* he, I would go.

Use the subjunctive also in a *that* clause when the main clause contains a verb of command, recommendation, or parliamentary motion:

I request that the defendant *have* a psychiatric examination.
I move that the meeting *be* adjourned.

The subjunctive is also used in certain idiomatic expressions:

Far *be* is for me to tell you how to raise your child.
If need *be*, I will finish the quilt by myself.

D. **Do Not Misuse Irregular Verb Forms.** Here are the standard principal parts (see G-3A above) of some common troublesome verbs. See your dictionary for others.

Present Tense	Past Tense	Past Participle
be [See G-4.2C]		
begin	began	begun
break	broke	broken
bring	brought	brought
choose	chose	chosen
(be)come	(be)came	(be)come
cost	cost	cost
do	did	done
drink	drank	drunk
drive	drove	driven
fall	fell	fallen

Present Tense	Past Tense	Past Participle
fly	flew	flown
forbid	forbade, forbad	forbidden
freeze	froze	frozen
give	gave	given
go	went	gone
grow	grew	grown
know	knew	known
lay [to put]	laid	laid
lead	led	led
lie [to rest]	lay	lain
lose	lost	lost
pay	paid	paid
ride	rode	ridden
ring	rang	rung
(a)rise	(a)rose	(a)risen
run	ran	run
say	said	said
see	saw	seen
shake	shook	shaken
shine [to give off light]	shone	shone

[*Shine*—to polish—is a different verb. It is regular.]

show	showed	shown, showed
sink	sank	sunk
speak	spoke	spoken
steal	stole	stolen
swim	swam	swum
swing	swung	swung
take	took	taken
tear	tore	torn
(a)wake	(a)woke, (a)waked	(a)waked, (a)woke(n)

[*Awaken* is a different verb. It is regular]

wear	wore	worn
write	wrote	written

E. Do Not Confuse Verbs Similar in Meaning or Spelling. Sometimes substituting a synonym for the verb that is puzzling you (such as *rest* for *lie* and *put* for *lay*) helps solve your puzzle. Many sets of troublesome verbs are explained in U, pages 74–92, including the following: *accept/except, adapt/adopt, affect/effect, brake/break, bring/take, can/may, cite/sight, emigrate/immigrate, hanged/hung, imply/infer, learn/teach, leave/let, lie/lay.*

G-5. Using Adjectives and Adverbs

Recall that an adjective modifies (describes or limits) a noun or occasionally a pronoun, and that an adverb modifies a verb or sometimes another modifier (adjective or adverb):

Adjectives: a *red* barn, a *swift* ride, a *happy* woman [descriptive];
             this isle, *seven* crowns, *some* cookies [limiting]
Adverbs: The horse ran *swiftly*. [modifying a verb, *ran*]
          The horse was *very* swift. [modifying an adjective, *swift*]
          The horse ran *very* swiftly. [modifying an adverb, *swiftly*]

Many adverbs are formed by the addition of *-ly* to adjectives: *smooth/smoothly, unforgettable/unforgettably*. An *-ly* ending thus usually signals an adverb—but not always, for *friendly, womanly,* and *saintly* are adjectives. A few common adverbs have the same form as their corresponding adjectives: *late, early, fast*. Some adverbs have two forms: *slow(ly), quick(ly)*. The sure way to tell an adjective from an adverb is to determine the word that it modifies:

You drive too *fast* [drive how? *fast:* adverb].
You are in the *fast* lane [which lane? *fast:* adjective].

The word *not* is an adverb.

1. Correct Use of Adjectives and Adverbs

A. Use an Adverb, Not an Adjective,

(1) *To modify an action verb:*

Wrong: He *sure* works hard.
Right: He *surely* works hard.

Wrong: He drives *crazy*.
Right: He drives *crazily*.

(2) *To modify an adjective:*

Wrong: This is a *real* fast car.
Right: This is a *really* fast car.

(3) *To modify another adverb:*

Wrong: She tries *awful* hard.
Right: She tries *extremely* hard.

B. Use an Adjective (as Subjective Complement) After a Linking Verb.

Janet is *jubilant*. [*Jubilant* describes *Janet*.]
She looks *happy*. [*Happy* describes *she*.]
The flowers smell *fragrant*. [*Fragrant* describes *flowers*.]

See G-4.2C, page 10, for an explanation and full list of linking verbs. Caution: Distinguish between a linking verb and the same verb used as an action verb.

C. Use *Good* and *Well, Bad* and *Badly* Correctly. Use *good* and *bad* (adjectives) as complements after a linking verb:

This book is *good.*
I feel *good.*
This fish tastes *bad.*

Use *well* and *badly* (adverbs) to modify an action verb:
She sings *well.*
I have failed *badly.*

NOTE: Well can be an adjective in the limited sense of "in good health":

I am feeling *well.*
She is not a *well* woman.

I feel good, on the other hand, refers to any kind of good feeling.

D. Use Comparative and Superlative Forms Correctly.

(1) *Most adjectives and adverbs have three degrees.* Notice how the *-er* and *-est* endings change the degree:

Positive (modifying one thing or action):
    My bed is *hard.*
    Your horse runs *fast.*
    This stone is *smooth.*
Comparative (comparing two):
    Your bed is the *harder* of the two.
    Your horse runs *faster* than mine.
    This stone is *smoother* than that one.
Superlative (comparing three or more):
    Of the three beds, his is the *hardest.*
    Your horse runs *fastest* of all.
    This stone is the *smoothest* one in the pile.

Some adjectives use *more* and *most* (or *less* and *least*) instead of *-er* and *-est.* Such adjectives sometimes have two syllables, but more often they have three syllables. Most adverbs also use *more, most, less,* and *least:*

Adjectives: beautiful, more beautiful, most beautiful
            intelligent, less intelligent, least intelligent
Adverbs: easily, more easily, most easily
        quietly, less quietly, least quietly

Some adjectives and adverbs use either form:

costly, costlier, costliest *or*
costly, more costly, most costly

(2) *A few adjectives and adverbs have irregular forms of comparison:*

good/well, better, best
bad/badly, worse, worst
many/much, more, most
little, less, least

(3) *Use the comparative (not the superlative) when comparing two things:*

Wrong: Of the two, Sybil is the *smartest*.
Right: Of the two, Sybil is the *smarter*.

2. Avoid These Errors in Adjective and Adverb Use.

A. Do Not Use Both Forms of the Comparative (*-er* and *More*) or of the Superlative (*-est* and *Most*) Together.
One form is enough:

Wrong: This car is *more faster* than that one.
Right: This car is *faster* than that one.

Wrong: Joan has the *most costliest* jewelry of any of us.
Right: Joan has the *most costly* jewelry of any of us.
Right: Joan has the *costliest* jewelry of any of us.

B. Do Not Compare Adjectives or Adverbs That Cannot Logically Be Compared, such as *unique, perfect, dead, empty, impossible, first, infinite*. A glass is either empty or not empty; it cannot be more or less empty (though it can be *nearly* empty):

Wrong: Our design was *more unique* than theirs. [*Unique* means "the only one of its kind"; things cannot be more or less unique.]
Right: Our design was *more nearly unique* than theirs.

G-6.   Using Pronouns

A pronoun substitutes for a noun, so that instead of saying *The team prided the team on the team's record,* we can say *The team prided **itself** on **its** record.* The noun that the pronoun substitutes for (stands for) is called its **antecedent**. *Team* is the antecedent of *itself* and *its*. (Not all kinds of pronouns have expressed antecedents.)

Pronouns share almost all the uses of nouns. (For those uses, see G-3.2, page 7.)

1. The Five Main Kinds of Pronouns

A. The Personal Pronouns. These designate one or more particular persons or things:

Person	Singular	Plural
FIRST [person(s) speaking]	I, my, mine, me	we, our, ours, us
SECOND [person(s) spoken to]	you, your, yours	you, your, yours
THIRD [any other person(s) or thing(s)]	he, his, him she, her, hers it, its	they, their, theirs, them

B. The Interrogative and Relative Pronouns

(1) The *interrogative pronouns* are *who (whose, whom), which, what.* They ask questions:

Who said that?
Whose car is that?
What is the time?
Which of the cars is his?
With *whom* did you speak?

(2) The *relative pronouns* are the same as the interrogative, plus *that* and the *-ever* forms: *whoever (whomever), whichever, whatever.* Relative pronouns introduce certain kinds of dependent clauses (sometimes called **relative clauses**):

The man *who called* was angry.
Chicago, *which I often visit,* is an exciting city.
I approve *whatever she decides.*

Use *who* for persons, *which* for things, and *that* for either:

Person: The officer *who* made the arrest was commended.
           The officer *that* made the arrest was commended.
Thing: California, *which* I love, is always sunny.
         The state *that* I love is always sunny.

NOTE: When *of which* sounds awkward, you may use *whose* with things:

We entered the harbor, *whose* pattern of sails and buoys delighted the eye.

C. The Demonstrative Pronouns are *this* (plural: *these*) and *that* (plural: *those*). They point out:

This is my house.
The ones I want are *these.*
That is Helen's house.
What kind of trees are *those?*

D. The Indefinite Pronouns refer to no particular person or thing:

Many will complain, but *few* will act; *most* will do *nothing.*
Someone must do *something,* but *no one* wants to do *anything.*

Here are some common indefinite pronouns:

one	someone	everyone
no one	somebody	anybody
everybody	nobody	something
anything	either	neither
all	any	both
some	few	many
most	another	others

NOTE: Closely related to the indefinite pronouns are the two **reciprocal** pronouns, *each other* and *one another.* See U, page 80.

E. The Reflexive and Intensive Pronouns are the *-self* forms of personal pronouns: *myself, yourself, yourselves, himself, herself, itself, ourselves, themselves.*

(1) *They are called reflexive when used as objects or as subjective complements:*

The teammates congratulated *themselves* on their victory. [object of verb]
She made a promise to *herself.* [object of preposition]
The boss is not *himself* today. [subjective complement]

(2) *They are called intensive when used as appositives, for emphasis:*

I *myself* am to blame.
Only they *themselves* are to blame.

Do not use a *-self* pronoun where a personal pronoun suffices:

Wrong: John and *myself* went.
Right: John and *I* went.

NOTE: There are no such words in standard English as *hisself, ourselfs, theirself, theirselves, yourselfs, themself, themselfs.*

2. Using the Right Pronoun Case.

The case of a pronoun is the form it takes in a particular use in a sentence (subject, direct object, etc.). English has three cases: **nominative, possessive,** and **objective.** The pronouns with different nominative and objective forms cause the most confusion: *I/me, he/him, she/her, we/us, they/them, who/whom.*

	Nominative Case (subject forms)	Possessive Case (possessive forms)	Objective Case (object forms)
Singular	I he, she, it	my, mine his, her, hers, its	me him, her, it
Plural	we they	our, ours their, theirs	us them
Singular and Plural	you who	your, yours whose	you whom

A. Nominative Case. Use the nominative (subject) forms—*I, he, she, we, they, who*—for

(1) *Subject: I* know it. *She* and *I* know it. *Who* knows it?

(2) *Subjective complement* (after linking verbs): The murderer is *she.*

NOTE: Although informal usage permits *It was her* or *It wasn't me,* most writers and speakers adhere to the nominative in formal usage: It was *she.* It was not *I.* This is *he.* See C(5) for pronoun case with the infinitive *to be.*

B. Objective Case. Use the distinctive object(ive) forms—*me, him, her, us, them, whom*—for any kind of object:

Direct object: We all greeted *him.*
Indirect object: We all gave *him* and *her* presents.
Object of preposition: We all gave a present to *her.*

C. Special Problems with Nominative and Objective Cases

(1) *A pronoun in a compound using* and *or* or *takes the same case* as it would if not compounded:

Wrong: *Him* and *me* can go. [Would you say *Him can go* or *Me can go?*]
Right: *He* and *I* can go. [*He* can go. *I* can go.]

Wrong: This gift is from Sally and *I.* [from *I?*]
Right: This gift is from Sally and *me.* [from *me*]

(2) *A pronoun followed by a noun appositive* takes the same case as it would if the noun were not there:

Wrong: *Us* girls want to thank you. [*Us* want . . . ?]
Right: *We* girls want to thank you. [*We* want . . .]

Wrong: He did it for *we* girls. [For *we?*]
Right: He did it for *us* girls. [He did it for *us.*]

(3) *A pronoun appositive* takes the same case as the word to which it is in apposition:

Two *people, you* and *she,* will go.
Father took *us—Jean* and *me—*downtown.
Let'*s* [Let *us*] *you* and *me* go to the store.

(4) *A pronoun in an incomplete comparison* takes the same case as it would if the comparison were complete:

Right: She found Sid sooner than *I* [did].
Right: She found Sid sooner than [she found] *me.*

(5) *A pronoun between a verb and an infinitive* (called the **subject of the infinitive**) takes the objective case:

I asked *him* to sing.
We wanted *them* to stay.

NOTE: If the infinitive *to be* has such a subject, any pronoun following *to be* also takes the objective case (since *be* takes the same case after it as before it):

They thought her to be *me.*
We wanted the winner to be *him.*

If *to be* does not have such a subject, any pronoun following *to be* takes the same case as the subject of the sentence (nominative):

The winner was thought to be *she.*

D. Possessive Case

(1) *Use the apostrophe ['] to form the possessive case of indefinite and reciprocal pronouns:* someone's, everybody's, each other's, no one's, etc.

(2) *Use the possessive case before a gerund:*

Wrong: We resented *him* leaving.
Right: We resented *his* leaving.

Wrong: The teacher objected to *them* singing in class.
Right: The teacher objected to *their* singing in class.

NOTE: A noun before a gerund also takes the possessive case:

Wrong: The teacher objected to the *students* singing in class.
Right: The teacher objected to the *students'* singing in class.
[plural possessive]

(3) *Do not use the apostrophe in the possessive case of personal pronouns* (his, hers, its, ours, yours, theirs) *or of* who (whose):

Whose book is this?
Is it *ours* or *theirs?*
It can't be *hers.*

It is a common error to confuse the possessives *its, whose, their,* and *your* with the contractions *it's (it is), who's (who is), they're (they are)* and *you're (you are).*

Remember that no possessive personal pronoun ever takes an apostrophe, nor does *whose:*

The dog wagged *its* tail. *Whose* dog is that?
The dogs wagged *their* tails. Is that *your* dog?

NOTE: To tell which form you need, mentally substitute the uncontracted form (*it is,* etc.). If it sounds right, you need the contraction:

(*Its/It's*) a fine day.→ *It is* a fine day.→ *It's* a fine day.
The tree shed (*its/it's*) leaves.→ The tree shed *it is* leaves? No.→The tree shed *its* leaves.

E. The Case of the Interrogative Pronouns *Who* and *Whom.* *Who* is nominative case; *whom* is objective:

Who came in first? [subject]
Whom did you meet?→You did meet *whom?* [direct object]
Whom did you go with?→You did go with *whom?* [object of preposition]

NOTE: When in doubt about using *who* or *whom,* try substituting *he* or *him.* If *he* sounds right, use *who;* if *him* sounds right, use *whom:*

(*Who/Whom*) rang the bell?→ *He* rang the bell. *Who* rang the bell?

(*Who/Whom*) did you see?→ You did see *him.*→ You did see *whom?*→ *Whom* did you see?

Although informal usage permits *Who did you see?* and *Who did you go with?* most careful writers adhere to *whom* in formal usage. Directly after a preposition, always use *whom:* With *whom* did you go?

F. The Case of a Relative Pronoun is determined by its use *within* its clause:

She is the one *who* scored the goal. [*Who* = subject of *scored.*]
She is the one *whom* we must stop. [*We must stop whom. Whom* = direct object of *must stop.*]
You must tell *whoever* comes. [*Whoever* = subject of *comes.*]
You must tell *whomever* you meet. [*Whomever* = direct object of *meet.*]
Go with *whoever* asks you. [*Whoever* = subject of *asks.*]

Do not be misled by other intervening clauses, such as *I think, it seems,* or *we are convinced.*

She is the one *who* I think *scored the goal.*
She is the one *whom* it is certain *we must stop.*

3. Avoiding Faulty Reference.
Be sure that each pronoun refers unmistakably only to its antecedent—the noun it stands for.

A. Ambiguous Reference occurs when a pronoun may refer to more than one noun. Clarify such ambiguity by rephrasing the sentence:

Wrong: Ms. Schatz has given the job to Ida because *she* knows what must be done. [Does *she* refer to Ms. Schatz or to Ida?]

Right: Ms. Schatz, *who* knows what must be done, has given Ida the job.
Right: Ms. Schatz has given the job to Ida, *who* knows what must be done.

Wrong: When the city negotiators met with the union representatives, *they* outlined *their* position.

Right: The city negotiators outlined *their* position when *they* met with the union representatives.

Right: The city negotiators met with the union representatives, *who* outlined *their* position.

B. Vague Reference occurs when a pronoun has no easily identifiable antecedent. Clarify the sentence by supplying the needed noun:

Wrong: In England *they* drive on the left. [Who are *they?*]
Right: The *English* drive on the left.

Wrong: At first, flying scared me because I had never been on *one.*
Right: At first, flying scared me because I had never been on *a plane.*

Avoid using *which, it, this,* or *that* to refer vaguely to a whole clause or sentence:

Wrong: The man had deliberately stepped on her toe, *which* bothered her. [Is it the man's act or her toe that bothers her?]

Right: The man's deliberate *stepping* on her toe bothered her.

Right: The man had deliberately stepped on her toe, *an act that* bothered her.

Wrong: The explorers canoed down the river and camped on a starlit beach. *It* was beautiful.

Right:The explorers canoed down the river and camped on a starlit beach. The *night* (or *river* or *beach*) was beautiful.

It is acceptable in *It is raining, It is a fine day,* etc.

G-7.   Recognizing Phrases

Being able to recognize phrases (and clauses) helps you avoid agreement errors, fragments, comma splices and fused sentences, and misplaced or dangling modifiers.

A **phrase** is a group of related words that is less than a sentence because it lacks a subject + verb. (Some phrases contain a part of a verb—a verbal.) A phrase usually functions as if it were a single word: noun, adjective, or adverb. For this reason it is important to think of and recognize phrases as units. There are two main kinds of phrases.

1. The Prepositional Phrase   is used chiefly as an adjective or adverb. It consists of a preposition + object (and possible modifiers of that object):

As adjective: The house *with the red shutters* is ours. [tells which house]
  The bird *in that tree* appears to be sleeping. [tells which bird]

As adverb: She died *in the old hospital.* [tells where]
  The boys did it *for a joke.* [tells why]

2. The Verbal Phrase.   There are three kinds: infinitive, gerund, and participial. (See G-4.3D, page 13, for explanation of these terms.)

A. An Infinitive Phrase consists of an infinitive + complement or modifiers or both:

As noun: *To become governor* is her aim. [subject]
  She wants *to become governor.* [direct object]

As adjective: I have a plan *to suggest to you.* [modifies *plan*]

As adverb: We ventured forth *to meet the foe.* [modifies *ventured*]
  Oscar is eager *to leave soon.* [modifies *eager*]

B. A Participial Phrase consists of a present or past participle + complement or modifiers or both. It is always used as an adjective:

The young man *reading a trashy novel* is my son. [modifies *man*]
Immersed in a trashy novel, the young man ignored his mother.
[modifies *man*]

Another kind of phrase using a participle is the **absolute phrase** (subject + participle + complement or modifiers or both), so called because it is grammatically independent of the sentence, though logically connected to it:

Her face reddening, Karen muttered an apology.
Karen muttered an apology, *her face reddening.*

Their bodies swaying, the audience listened to the music.
The audience listened to the music, *their bodies swaying.*

C. A Gerund Phrase consists of the *-ing* form + complement or modifiers or both. It is always used as a noun:

Reading a trashy novel is a waste of time. [subject]
How can you enjoy *reading a trashy novel*? [direct object]
His chief pastime is *reading a trashy novel*. [subjective complement]
He relaxes by *reading a trashy novel*. [object of preposition]

For avoidance of dangling or misplaced phrases, see G-10.2C(2), D, pages 35, 36.

NOTE: Some authorities use the term **noun phrase** to refer to a noun and its modifiers (*the five old men in their wheelchairs*), and **verb phrase** for a main verb and its auxiliaries (*might have been drinking*). See G-4.2D, page 10.

G-8.   Recognizing Clauses

A **clause** is a group of related words containing a subject + verb. There are two kinds: **independent (main)** and **dependent (subordinate).**

1. Kinds of Clauses

A. An Independent Clause sounds complete and makes sense when it stands alone. Every simple sentence is an independent clause; however, the term *clause* usually refers to such a word group as part of a larger sentence:

I found the key, and *I gave it to Helen.*
We waxed our skis, but *it never snowed.*
She admired him greatly, for *he was a genius.*

B. A Dependent Clause, though it contains a subject + verb, cannot stand alone grammatically. What makes a clause dependent is a connecting word that forces the clause to be linked to an independent clause:

[dependent clause in *italics;* connecting word in ***bold italics***]

We will cheer ***when*** *the space shuttle touches down.*
I recognized the scarf ***that*** *she was wearing.*
Because *I was right,* I refused to apologize.
I refused to apologize ***because*** *I was right.*

2. Kinds of Dependent Clauses

A. An Adjective Clause functions as an adjective, modifying a noun or pronoun. It is introduced and connected to the independent clause by the relative pronoun *who (whose, whom), which,* or *that,* or sometimes by *when, where,* or *why:*

The boy *that applied first* was hired. [modifies *boy*]
We greeted everyone *who arrived.* [modifies *everyone*]
Let's catch the bus, *which will take us home.* [modifies *bus*]

Adjective clauses are either **restrictive** or **nonrestrictive**, depending on their necessity in the sentence. See P-1.1E(2), page 41, for explanation and punctuation.

B. An Adverb Clause functions as an adverb, modifying a verb, adjective, or other adverb. It tells *when, where, how, why, under what condition, with what result,* or *to what degree.* It is introduced and connected to the independent clause by a subordinate conjunction, such as the ones listed below.

Adverb Clause Telling	Introduced by Subordinate Conjunction	Example
Time [*when?*]	when(ever), while, after, before, since, as, as soon as, until	I left *before Jo returned.*
Place [*where?*]	where, wherever	We went *where the land was fertile.*
Manner [*how?*]	as, as if, as though	He walks *as if he's dazed.*
Cause [*why?*]	because, since	I left *because I was angry.*
Purpose [*why?*]	(so) that, in order that	She came *so that she might help.*
Concession [*under what condition?*]	(al)though, even though	They came, *although they were tired.*
Condition [*under what condition?*]	if, unless, whether, provided	You can go *if you leave early.*
Result [*that what resulted?*]	that	He ran so fast *that he was exhausted.*
Comparison [*to what degree?*]	as, than	She is taller *than I* [*am*].

Most adverb clauses can shift to the beginning of the sentence:

If you leave early, you can go.
Before Jo returned, I left.
Because I was hungry, I ate quickly.

C. **A Noun Clause** functions as a noun. It is introduced and connected to the independent clause by the relative pronoun *who(ever), which-(ever), what(ever),* or *that* or by *when, where, why, how,* or *whether:*

What they did made little sense. [subject]
I know *that he went.* [direct object]
Give *whoever answers the door* this note. [indirect object]
Give this note to *whoever answers the door.* [object of preposition]

3. **Clauses in Sentences.** Sentences can be classified according to their structure—that is, the number and kind(s) of clauses they have. There are four kinds of sentences:

A. **The Simple Sentence** (one independent clause):

The door opened.
The speeding car careened around the corner.
In the morning the executives jog around the track.

B. **The Compound Sentence** (two or more independent clauses):

The door opened, and *our guests entered.*
The clock struck eight, the door opened, and *our guests entered.*
Our guests arrived at eight; dinner was to be served at nine.

C. **The Complex Sentence** (one independent clause + one or more dependent clauses):

[dependent clause in **bold**]

As the clock struck eight, *the door opened.*
My heart jumped **when the speeding car careened around the corner.**
After the executives jog around the track, *they go to work refreshed.*

D. **The Compound-Complex Sentence** (a compound sentence + one or more dependent clauses):

As the clock struck eight, *the door opened* and *our guests entered.*
My heart jumped but *I couldn't move* **when the speeding car careened around the corner.**
Before they go to work in the morning, *some of the executives jog* and *others swim.*

G-9. Agreement

In sentences, subjects and verbs have matching forms to show their grammatical relation. So do pronouns and their antecedents. This relation is called **agreement.**

1. Make Every Verb Agree with Its Subject in Person and Number.

A. **There Are Three Grammatical Persons:** the **first person** [the person(s) speaking: *I, we*], the **second person** [the person(s) being spoken to: *you*], and the **third person** [the person(s) being spoken about: *he, she, it, they,* and any noun]. In most verbs, only the third person present tense singular has a special form: the ending *-s. I run, we run,* and *you run,* but *he* or *she* run**s**. The verb *be* is special:

PERSON	PRESENT TENSE	PAST TENSE
First	I am, we are	I was, we were
Second	you are	you were
Third	he *or* she is	he *or* she was
	they are	they were

Use the verb form that matches the person of the subject.

Wrong: You is late.
Right: You are late.

NOTE: When two or more subjects in different persons are joined by *or,* the verb agrees with the subject nearer to it:

Either she or I *am* going.
Either she or they *are* going.
Neither the twins nor Bob *is* going.

B. **There Are Two Grammatical Numbers: singular** (referring to one thing) and **plural** (referring to more than one). Singular subjects must take singular verbs; plural subjects must take plural verbs. Except for *be* (see A above), only the third person singular in the present and present perfect tenses presents a problem, because of its *-s* ending:

[singular in **bold;** plural in *italics*]

Wrong: **Jo** *like* tacos. **She** *don't* [*do not*] like pizza.
Right: **Jo likes** tacos. **She doesn't** [**does not**] like pizza.

C. **Intervening Word Groups.** Make subject and verb agree regardless of phrases or clauses between them:

Phrase: The *collection* (of rare books) *is* lost.

A *man* (from the cleaners) *is* here.

Clause: The *woman* (who owns these horses) *lives* here.

The *actors* (that starred in the movie) *have* come.

Parenthetical phrases introduced by (*together*) *with, like, as well as, including, in addition to,* etc. do not affect the number of the actual subject:

Elizabeth, together with her friends, *is* coming.
The *boys,* as well as their father, *have* arrived.

D. Two or More Subjects

(1) *Joined by* and. Use a plural verb:

A book and a pencil **are** all I need.
Are *chemistry and history* **required?**

However, if both subjects refer to a single person or thing, use a singular verb:

My friend and benefactor **is** here. [One person is both friend and benefactor.]
Scotch and soda **is** my favorite drink. [one drink]
Black beans and rice **is** a popular Cuban dish.

Use a singular verb when *each* or *every* precedes the subjects:

Every man and every woman **is expected** to pay.
Each photographer and each correspondent **was** responsible for covering a section of the war zone.

(2) *Joined by* or *or* nor. Make the verb agree with the nearer subject:

Bettina or Sharon **is going** with you.
The Giants or the Dodgers **are going** to finish first.
Bettina or the twins **are going** with you.
The twins or Bettina **is going** with you.

E. Singular Pronouns.
Use a singular verb when the subject is the singular indefinite pronoun *one, each, either, neither, everyone, everybody, anyone, anybody, someone, somebody, no one,* or *nobody:*

Each of them **wants** me to stay.
Everyone in all our dorms **is** going home.

After *all, any, most, none, some,* or *such,* use either a singular or a plural verb, depending on whether the pronoun refers to something singular or plural:

The milk was left in the sun; *all* of it **has turned** sour.
The guests became bored; *all* **have left.**
Such **were** the joys of youth.
Such **is** the way of the world.

F. Collective Nouns.
Use a singular verb when thinking of the group as a unit:

A new *family* **has moved** next door.

Use a plural verb when thinking of the group members as individuals:

The new *family* **have been fighting** with one another.

NOTE: In American English, many authorities prefer the following:

The *members* of the new family **have been fighting** with one another.

G. Linking Verbs. Make a linking verb agree with its subject, not its subjective complement:

Books **are** her chief interest. Her chief *interest* **is** books.

H. Singular Nouns in Plural Form. Such nouns as *news, billiards, whereabouts, athletics, measles, mumps, mathematics,* and *economics* are logically singular. Use a singular verb:

Her *whereabouts* **is** unknown.
Measles **has been** nearly **eliminated.**

However, use a plural verb with two-part objects such as *trousers, pants, pliers, scissors, tweezers:*

The *tweezers* **are** not useful for this; perhaps the *pliers* **are.**

I. *There* and *It* as Expletives (words with no meaning in a sentence):

   (1) *There* is never the subject. In sentences beginning with *there is (was)* or *there are (were),* look *after* the verb for the subject, and make the verb agree with the subject:

      There **is** a *bee* in your bonnet. [A bee is in your bonnet.]
      There **are** *bats* in your belfry. [Bats are in your belfry.]
      There **were** *a man and a dog* in the car.

   (2) *It,* on the other hand, is always singular:

      It **was** Aunt Diane who telephoned.
      It **was** the boys who telephoned.

J. Literary Titles and Words Considered as Words are always singular:

The Ambassadors **is** not a light novel.
Children **is** an irregular plural noun.

K. Sums of Money and Measurements. When considering a sum as a single item, use a singular verb:

Ten dollars **is** not much money these days.
Five gallons **is** the capacity of this tank.

When considering individual dollars, gallons, miles, etc., use a plural verb:

The *dollars* **were** neatly arranged in stacks.
Gallons of gasoline **are** spilling from the tank.

In an arithmetic problem, you may use either:

Six and four **is [makes]** ten. *Six and four* **are [make]** ten.

NOTE: *The number* takes a singular verb; *a number,* plural:

    The number of people who get measles **is** increasing.
    A number of voters always **turn** out for the governor's election.

L. Relative Pronouns. Use a singular verb if the antecedent of *who, which,* or *that* is singular; use a plural verb if the antecedent is plural:

She is the only *member* **who smokes.** *[Antecedent of who is member.]*

She is one of the *members* **who smoke.** [Antecedent of *who* is *members.*]

It is *I* **who am responsible.** [Antecedent of *who* is *I.*]

2. Make Every Pronoun Agree with Its Antecedent in Person and Number.

A. Avoid Illogical Shifts to *You.*

Wrong: *I* like swimming because it gives **you** firm muscles.
Right: *I* like swimming because it gives **me** firm muscles.

Wrong: If *a person* eats just before swimming, **you** may get a cramp.
Right: If *a person* eats just before swimming, **he** or **she** may get a cramp.

B. Singular Pronouns.
Use a singular pronoun when referring to antecedents such as *person, man, woman, one, anyone, anybody, someone, somebody, either, neither, each, everyone, everybody:*

A person should know what **he** wants in life.
Neither of the women will state **her** preference.
Everyone has **her** own opinion about the plan.

NOTE: When a singular antecedent (such as *student, citizen*) may be of mixed gender, you have three choices:

    (1)   Use the masculine pronoun: Every student raised **his** hand.
    (2)   Use both pronouns: Every student raised **his** or **her** hand.
    (3)   Change the sentence to plural: All the students raised **their** hands.

Many people consider choice 1 sexist and choice 2 awkward; when it is possible and not inconsistent with surrounding sentences, choice 3 is usually best.

C. Antecedents Joined by *and, or,* and *nor.*
Follow the same principles as for subject–verb agreement (see 1D above).

    (1) *With antecedents joined by* and, *use a plural pronoun:*

        Bettina and Sharon are performing **their** act.
        Tod and I are going to **our** grandparents' house for Thanksgiving.

    (2) *With antecedents joined by* or *or* nor, *make the pronoun agree with the nearer antecedent:*

        Either Bettina or Sharon will perform **her** act.
        The Giants or the Dodgers should win **their** divisional title.
        Either Bettina or the twins will perform **their** act.

D. Collective Nouns. Follow the same principle as for subject–verb agreement (see 1F above); let the meaning of the noun determine the number of the pronoun:

The *family* has moved into **its** new home.
The *family* have settled **their** differences.

E. Demonstrative Pronouns Used as Adjectives. Make *this, that, these,* or *those* agree with the noun it modifies:

Wrong: I like *these kind* of fish. [*These* is plural; *kind,* singular.]
Right: I like *this kind* of fish.
     I like *these kinds* of fish.

G-10.   Effective Sentences

Good sentences reflect clear thinking. A clumsy sentence says that an idea has been poorly thought out. Consider, therefore, not only what you want to say, but also how you can best say it. A well-written sentence has **unity, coherence,** and **emphasis.** Unity and coherence make it logical and clear; emphasis makes it forceful.

1. Follow These Guidelines to Write More Effective Sentences.

A. Vary Sentence Length. A short, simple sentence can be forceful: *The queen is dead.* But a string of short sentences usually gives a choppy, childish effect: *I walked through the woods. I saw a squirrel. It darted up a tree.* Combining sentences that have related ideas clarifies the relation and relative importance of the ideas. Sections B–D below describe some combining techniques.

B. Use Coordination. You can regard related simple sentences as independent clauses and join them with a comma and a coordinate conjunction to form a compound sentence:

Choppy: The day dawned clear. We took our umbrellas.
Better: The day dawned clear, *but* we took our umbrellas. [The conjunction *but* shows the contrast between the two facts.]

Weak: We walked to work. The day was sunny.
Better: We walked to work, *for* the day was sunny. [The conjunction *for* shows that one fact caused the other.]

Choppy: French class met at noon. Art met at two.
Better: French class met at noon, *and* art met at two. [The *and* adds little meaning, but the one longer sentence reads more smoothly than the two shorter ones.]

NOTE: Although joining equally important clauses with coordinate conjunctions can be effective, using too many *and*'s or *so*'s offers little if any improvement over the string of short simple sentences you are trying to avoid. As alternatives, consider compounding and subordination, below.

C. Use Compounding. Combine simple sentences that have the same subjects or verbs so that you have only one sentence, with a compound subject or predicate:

Weak: Carol is learning tennis. I am learning tennis, too.
Better: [*Both*] *Carol and I* are learning tennis.

NOTE: Check subject–verb agreement as you rewrite using compounding:

Weak: We put up the tent. We fell asleep at once.
Better: We *put* up the tent *and fell* asleep at once.

NOTE: Ordinarily there is no comma between the parts of a compound predicate.

D. Use Subordination. In combining simple sentences, you can emphasize one by subordinating the other—reducing it to a dependent clause. By doing so you usually express the relation between ideas more clearly than by coordination or compounding:

Weak: The sun came out. Sally headed for the beach.
Clear: *When* the sun came out, Sally headed for the beach. [*When* stresses the time connection between the two facts.]
Clear: Sally headed for the beach *because* the sun came out. [*Because* stresses the causal connection between the two facts.]
Clear: Sally, *who* was glad to see the sun come out, headed for the beach. [The idea in the *who* clause is reduced to secondary importance.]

Be careful not to subordinate the *main* idea—the one you would mention if you could mention only one:

Wrong: President Kennedy, *who was shot dead,* was riding in an open car.
Right: *President Kennedy,* who was riding in an open car, *was shot dead.*

For a fuller discussion of subordination, see G-8, page 25.

E. Use Reduction. Wherever possible, eliminate needless words by reducing clauses to phrases and phrases to single words:

Wordy (clause): *Because she was discouraged about writing stories,* Erika decided to try nonfiction.
Tighter (phrase): *Discouraged about writing stories,* Erika decided to try nonfiction.

Wordy (clause): The person *who is holding the pistol* is the starter.
Tighter (phrase): The person *holding the pistol* is the starter.

Wordy (phrase): She is a child *possessed of talent.*
Tighter (word): She is a *talented* child.

NOTE: Use caution in placing modifiers; see 2C(2), (3) and 2D below.

F. **Use Parallel Structure** (the same grammatical form) with two or more coordinate expressions, in comparisons, and with correlative conjunctions:

Wrong: Kay is *vivacious* [adjective], *with keen wit* [prepositional phrase], and *has a friendly manner* [verb + complement].
Right: Kay is *vivacious, keen-witted,* and *friendly* [all adjectives].

Wrong: Arthur likes *drinking* and *to gamble.*
Right: Arthur likes *drinking* and *gambling* [or *to drink* and *to gamble*].

Wrong: Arthur likes *gambling* more than *to drink.*
Right: Arthur likes *gambling* more than *drinking.*

Wrong: Jo **not only** *likes* [verb] dogs **but also** *cats* [noun].
Right: Jo likes **not only** *dogs* [noun] **but also** *cats* [noun].

2. Avoid These Faults in Sentence Construction.

A. **Fragments.** A **fragment** is a piece of a sentence, such as a phrase or dependent clause, erroneously punctuated as if it were a complete sentence. When you discover a fragment in your writing, either (1) attach the fragment to an independent clause or (2) rewrite the fragment to form a sentence by itself. Even a statement with a subject and a predicate can be a fragment if it follows a subordinate conjunction, such as *if, when,* or *because.* In the incorrect examples below, the fragments are in italics:

Wrong: I was happy. *Because finals were over.*
Right: I was happy *because finals were over.* [fragment attached to independent clause]

Wrong: *Walking across the campus.* Ada slipped and fell.
Right: *Walking across the campus,* Ada slipped and fell.

Wrong: *An idea that appealed to us.*
Right: *The idea appealed to us.* [fragment rewritten as a sentence by itself]

B. **Comma Splices and Fused Sentences.** A **comma splice** is the erroneous joining of independent clauses with a comma rather than a conjunction or semicolon.

Wrong: The day was stifling, it made me sluggish.
Wrong: The Seahawks won easily, they had superior coaching.

A **fused sentence** is the erroneous joining of independent clauses with no conjunction or punctuation at all:

Wrong: The day was stifling it made me sluggish.
Wrong: The Seahawks won easily they had superior coaching.

To avoid such errors (both also called **run-ons** or **run-togethers**), first be sure that you can recognize an independent clause. Review G-8.1A, page 25, if necessary. Next, learn these four ways to correct run-ons. Choose the way that best fits your purpose and your paragraph.

(1) *Separate the clauses into two sentences:*

Right: The day was stifling. It made me sluggish.

This is the simplest but rarely the best way, for too many short sentences make your writing sound choppy and immature. Moreover, you fail to specify a relation between the ideas in the clauses. If your purpose is to give equal emphasis to the two ideas, however, this way can be effective:

Right: The Seahawks won easily. They had superior coaching.

(2) *Join the clauses with a coordinating conjunction:*

Right: The day was stifling, *and* it made me sluggish.

This is often a better way than making separate sentences, but you must not overuse this either. *And,* especially, shows only a very general relation between ideas. The sentence below shows a more specific relation between the ideas:

Right: The day made me sluggish, *for* it was stifling.

(3) *Join the clauses with a semicolon:*

Right: The day was stifling; it made me sluggish.
Right: The Seahawks won easily; they had superior coaching.

A semicolon can give your writing a formal tone; it is often effective in balanced sentences, such as *Today was delightful; yesterday was dreadful.*

(4) *Join the clauses by making one of them a dependent (subordinate) clause.* Join them with subordinate conjunctions, such as *because, if, when, since, after, although,* and *unless,* or with relative pronouns: *who(m), which, that.* Subordinating is often the best way to eliminate run-ons, since the kinds of words listed here show the precise relation between ideas:

Right: I felt sluggish *because the day was stifling.*
Right: The Seahawks, *who had superior coaching,* won decisively.

For more on subordination, see G-8.1B, 2, pages 25–26, and G-10.1D, page 33.

C. Needless Separation of Related Parts of a Sentence

(1) *Do not needlessly separate subject and verb or verb and complement:*

Wrong: *I,* hoping very much to see him, *hurried.*
Right: Hoping very much to see him, *I hurried.*

(2) *Place modifying words, phrases, and clauses as close as possible to the words they modify:*

- **Adverb:**

Wrong: What great luck! I *almost* **won** $1,000 in the lottery. [*Almost won* means that you came close but did not win anything.]
Right: What great luck! I won *almost* **$1,000** in the lottery. [You won nearly $1,000.]

Only, nearly, scarcely, hardly, just, and *even* present the same problem.

- **Phrase:**

Wrong: Notify us if you can **stay** *on the enclosed card.*
Right: **Notify** us *on the enclosed card* if you can stay. [*On the enclosed card* should modify *notify,* not *stay.*]
Wrong: *Floating inside the bottle,* **Ms. Fleisch** saw some mysterious specks.
Right: Ms. Fleisch saw some mysterious **specks** *floating inside the bottle.*

- **Clause:**

Wrong: Ann put a hat on her **head** *that she had just bought.*
Right: On her head Ann put a **hat** *that she had just bought.*

(3) *Avoid "squinting" modifiers.* A squinting modifier comes between two verbs so that the reader cannot tell to which verb it refers:

Wrong: Mark **decided** *after his vacation* to **see** a doctor.
Right: Mark decided to **see** a doctor *after his vacation.*
Right: *After his vacation* Mark **decided** to see a doctor.

(4) *Avoid awkward splitting of infinitives.* The two parts of an infinitive belong together; avoid putting words between them unless your sentence would otherwise be unclear or sound odd:

Poor: I asked her *to* from time to time *visit* me.
Better: I asked her *to visit* me from time to time.

(5) *In formal English, avoid ending a sentence with a preposition unless the sentence would otherwise sound awkward:*

Informal: Sculpture is one art [*which*] she excelled *at.*
Formal: Sculpture is one art *at which* she excelled.

D. Dangling Modifiers. A modifier (usually a phrase) "dangles" when there is no word in the sentence that it can sensibly modify. Correct a dangling modifier in any of the ways shown below.

(1) *Dangling participle:*

Wrong: *Flying over Switzerland,* the jagged **Alps** appeared awesome. [The nearest noun to the phrase should name the person doing the flying. Instead, the sentence seems to say that the Alps were flying.]

Right: *Flying over Switzerland,* **Pat** was awed by the jagged Alps. [correct noun put nearest to phrase]

Right: *As* **Pat flew** *over Switzerland,* the jagged Alps awed him. [phrase expanded into a clause]

(2) *Dangling gerund:*

Wrong: *After walking for hours,* the **cabin** appeared in the distance.

Right: *After walking for hours,* the **hikers** saw the cabin in the distance.

Right: *After the* **hikers had walked** *for hours,* the cabin appeared in the distance.

(3) *Dangling infinitive:*

Wrong: *To be well cooked,* **you** must boil beets for half an hour.

Right: *To be well cooked,* **beets** must be boiled for half an hour.

(4) *Dangling elliptical clause.* An elliptical clause is one from which the subject and all or part of the verb have been dropped as understood, e.g., *while* [I was] *skiing in Utah:*

Wrong: *While still a toddler,* my **father** gave me swimming lessons.

Right: *While* **I was** *still a toddler,* my father gave me swimming lessons.

Right: *While still a toddler,* I was given swimming lessons by my father.

Ellipsis is permissible only when the subject of both clauses is the same, as in the last example above (*I* is the understood subject of the elliptical clause).

E. Incomplete Comparisons or Expressions of Degree

Wrong: I felt *so* sad.
Right: I felt *so* sad that I cried.

Wrong: Salaries of airline executives are higher *than* pilots.
Right: Salaries of airline executives are higher *than those of* pilots.

F. Needless Shifts

(1) *In number:*

Wrong: If *a person* works hard, *they* will succeed.
Right: If *a person* works hard, *she* will succeed.
Right: If *people* work hard, *they* will succeed.

This is a matter of agreement; see G-9.2B, page 31.

(2) *In person:*

Wrong: If *a person* works hard, *you* will succeed.

See the correct sentences in (1) above. Also see G-9.2A, page 31.

(3) *In subject or voice of verb:*

Wrong: As *we approached* the house, *laughter could be heard.* [*Approached* is active; *could be heard,* passive. Subject shifts from *we* to *laughter.*]
Right: As *we approached* the house, *we could hear* laughter.

(4) *In tense of verb.* See G-4.4A, page 14.

(5) *In mood of verb:*

Wrong: *Finish* your work, and then you *should rest.* [*Finish* is imperative in mood; *should rest,* indicative.]
Right: *Finish* your work, and then *rest.*

G. Faulty Predication. See U, pages 84 and 87, under *is when, is where* and *reason is because.*

H. Redundant or Inflated Wording

(1) *Redundancy* (needless repetition) in general:

Wrong: In this book it states that we have an *absolutely* unique town hall. *This town hall* is the tallest *in height* in the nation. *In my opinion, I think* that we should be proud of that.
Right: This book states that we have a unique town hall, the tallest in the nation. We should be proud of that.

(2) *Double negatives:*

Wrong: I *can't hardly* hear you. [*Hardly, barely,* and *scarcely* mean *almost not,* and thus act as negatives.]
Right: I *can hardly* hear you.
     I *can't* hear you.

(3) *Superfluous **that**:*

Wrong: We know *that,* although we won, *that* we won't get the prize.
Right: We know *that,* although we won, we won't get the prize.

(4) *Inflated or obscure phrasing.* Avoid elaborate modifiers and unnecessary Latinate diction (words with endings such as *-tion, -ity, -ize,* or *-ify*). Avoid also useless suffixes (as in *zealousness* for *zeal*); unfamiliar foreign phrases; and needless, unexplained jargon (technical or other terms that the general reader would not know, such as *multi-modality approach to ESL*).

Express your ideas in clear, direct language. By all means, try to increase your vocabulary, but use words with accuracy and intent to convey meaning, not merely to impress your reader. Otherwise, your writing may appear affected, and you may even obscure your ideas:

Inflated: Individuals who have undergone the training process in emergency rescue procedures have in numerous situations demonstrated the ability to implement such techniques in the prevention of fatalities from accidents occurring within their own dwelling units.

Better: People trained in emergency rescuing have often been able to save lives in accidents in their own homes.

PUNCTUATION

Punctuation marks are the traffic signals of writing. Without punctuation, many a written passage would become as chaotic as a large city without traffic lights. The writer's use of punctuation assists the reader through the heavy traffic of ideas that a written passage may contain.

Some punctuation marks *separate* words or ideas; others *emphasize* them; still others *group* and *keep together* related ideas. In all, punctuation marks clarify written material that would otherwise confuse and perhaps mislead.

Most punctuation rules are not difficult to master. Careful writers learn these rules and tend to conform to the established pattern of punctuation, reserving their originality not for devising their own mode of punctuation but for choosing and arranging the words with which they convey their ideas.

P-1.   The Comma [,]

Misuse of the comma accounts for about half of all punctuation errors. Carefully studying the following rules should enable you to punctuate more clearly and effectively.

1. Use a Comma to Set Off

A. Independent (Main) Clauses. A comma follows the first of two independent clauses that are joined by coordinate conjunctions (*and, but, or, nor, for, yet, so*):

The play's star is Glenda Glimmer, *and* its author is Tennessee Miller.

Miller's early plays were widely acclaimed, *but* his more recent ones have failed.

Do *not* use a comma

- If there is no full clause (subject + verb) after the conjunction:

Wrong: George straightened his tie, *and* put on his jacket.
Right: George straightened his tie *and* put on his jacket.

- *After* the conjunction:

Wrong: I ordered chicken *but,* he ordered lobster.
Right: I ordered chicken, *but* he ordered lobster.

41

- Between very short independent clauses:

  Wrong: He lies, and she cheats.
  Right: He lies and she cheats.

- Between independent clauses not joined by a coordinate conjunction (use a semicolon instead):

  Wrong: The starting gun sounded, the crowd roared.
  Right: The starting gun sounded; the crowd roared.

  See comma splices and fused sentences, G-10.2B, page 34.

B. Introductory Elements

(1) *An introductory adverb clause:*

If you pay full tuition now, you may register by mail.

NOTE: Usually you need no comma when the adverb clause follows the main clause: You may register by mail *if you pay full tuition now.*

(2) *A long prepositional phrase or a series of prepositional phrases:*

In the cool air of that April morning, we strolled along the boulevard.

NOTE: Unless clarity demands one, you do not need a comma after one short introductory phrase: *In the morning* we strolled along the boulevard.

(3) *A verbal phrase:*

Speaking off the record, the mayor admitted the error.
To play bridge well, you need a good memory.
By playing bridge every week, Stella sharpened her mind.

An infinitive or gerund phrase used as the *subject* of a sentence is not an introductory element. Do not set it off:

To play bridge well is my ambition.
Playing bridge every week sharpened Stella's mind.

C. Items in a Series.
Use commas to separate words, phrases, or clauses in a series of three or more:

Words: I enjoy the old films of *Bogart, Cagney, Garbo,* and *Hepburn.*
Phrases: The book is available *in bookstores, at newsstands,* or *by mail.*
Clauses: *She took French lessons, she studied guidebooks,* and *she talked to people who had been to Paris.*

NOTE: Some writers omit the comma before *and* or *or* in a series. Including this comma, however, ensures clarity.
    Use a comma before *etc.* at the end of a series: pork, beans, *etc.*

Do *not* use a comma

- With only two items: Ed bought *spaghetti and pork.*

- When you repeat *and* or *or* between every two items: Ed bought spaghetti *and* pancake mix *and* pork.

- Before the first item or after the last item:

Wrong: Ed *bought, spaghetti,* pancake mix, and pork.
Right: Ed *bought spaghetti,* pancake mix, and pork.

Wrong: Spaghetti, pancakes, and *pork, are* not everyone's favorites.
Right: Spaghetti, pancakes, and *pork are* not everyone's favorites.

D. **Coordinate Adjectives.** In a series of two or more, use commas to separate adjectives of equal importance. Do not put a comma after the last adjective:

Tall, stately trees lined the roadway.
Vulgar, snide, or *obscene* remarks are not appreciated here.

NOTE: Certain combinations of adjectives flow naturally together and need no commas: *little red* schoolhouse; *five funny old* men; *additional monetary* demands. Determining when to omit commas is tricky, but generally, if the adjectives sound odd in a different order (*red little* schoolhouse, *old funny five* men, *monetary additional* demands), you probably should omit commas.

E. **Parenthetical Expressions.** These are words or word groups that interrupt the main flow of thought in a sentence and are not essential to the meaning of the sentence.

(1) *General parenthetical expressions:*

She was, *in my opinion,* outstanding.
He, *on the other hand,* performed unconvincingly.
The entire production, *moreover,* lacked vitality.
It is unfortunate, *to be sure.* [Note the vast difference in meaning from *It is unfortunate to be sure.*]

Other common parenthetical expressions include *as a matter of fact, to tell the truth, of course, incidentally, namely, in the first place, therefore, thus, consequently, however, nevertheless.*

NOTE: Not all these expressions are always set off. You may choose not to set off *perhaps, likewise, at least, indeed, therefore, thus,* and certain others in sentences where you feel they do not interrupt your thought flow:

We may, *perhaps,* have been harsh in firing Jenkins.
We may *perhaps* have been harsh in firing Jenkins.

See P-5B, page 47, for other punctuation with *therefore, however,* and other conjunctive adverbs.

(2) *Nonrestrictive (nonessential) clauses.* A **nonrestrictive** clause (usually beginning with *which* or a form of *who*) is parenthetical. The information it gives is *not* essential to the meaning of the sentence. Being parenthetical, such a clause is set off within commas:

Parsons Boulevard, *which runs past my home,* is being repaved.
Penny Prentiss, *who lives in Hill Hall,* has won the award.

A **restrictive** clause *is* essential to the meaning of the sentence. It identifies a preceding noun; it answers the question "which one?" Such a clause is written without commas:

The street *which runs past my home* is being repaved.
A woman *who lives in Hill Hall* has won the award.

These restrictive clauses tell *which* street and *which* woman. Without the clauses the sentences could refer to any street or any woman. There is an easy test to distinguish restrictive from nonrestrictive clauses. A restrictive clause will sound right if you substitute *that* for *who* or *which;* a nonrestrictive clause will not:

Sounds right: A woman *that lives in Hill Hall* has won the award. [Test works; clause is restrictive. Omit commas.]
Sounds wrong: Penny Prentiss *that lives in Hill Hall* has won the award. [Test fails; clause is nonrestrictive. Use commas (and *who*).]

(3) *Nonrestrictive (nonessential) phrases.* Follow the principle for nonrestrictive clauses (see (2) above):

Restrictive: The woman *wearing red* is Jack's sister.
Nonrestrictive: Ms. Atlee, *wearing red,* is Jack's sister.
Restrictive: The locker *with the Yosemite poster* is mine.
Nonrestrictive: Locker 356, *with the Yosemite poster,* is mine.

(4) *Most appositives:*

America's greatest playwright, *Eugene O'Neill,* was once a sailor.
The hermit crab, *a South Pacific species,* seals itself into its home for life.

NOTE: Some appositives are restrictive and take no commas:

The playwright *Eugene O'Neill* was once a sailor.
I wrote to my daughter *Ella.* [one of several daughters]

F. Absolute phrases

The day being warm, we headed for the beach.
Bosley, *his clothes hanging in tatters*, staggered into camp.

G. Names or Other Words Used in Direct Address

Henry, what are you doing?
For my encore, *ladies and gentlemen,* I will play *Träumerei.*

H. *Yes* and *No* at the Beginning of a Sentence

Yes, we have neckties on sale.

I. Mild Interjections (expressions of less than strong emotion):

Well, I'll have to think that over.
Oh, what did she say?

NOTE: Strong interjections take exclamation points: *No!* I can't believe it.

J. Direct Quotations. Generally, use one or more commas to separate a direct quotation from preceding or following words:

"I love you," she whispered.
"And I," he replied, "love you."

Punctuation of quotations is treated fully in P-8, page 51.

K. Examples Introduced by *Such as, Especially, Particularly;* Expressions of Contrast

Ira enjoys all crafts, *especially* wood carving.
On weekends we offer several courses, *such as* Biology 101 and Music 210, for nontraditional students.
Dresden lies in Germany, *not* Poland.

NOTE: Some *such as* phrases are restrictive: Days *such as* this are rare.

2. Use a Comma Also

A. In Place of Omitted or Understood Words

Shirley attends Harvard; *her brother, Yale.*

B. Before a Confirmatory Question

It's a warm day, *isn't it?*

C. In Letters

(1) *After the greeting in a friendly letter: Dear Mabel,*

NOTE: Use a colon after the greeting in a business letter: *Dear Ms. Worth:*

(2) *After the complimentary close in all letters: Very truly yours,*

D. In Dates and Addresses.
In a month-day-year date, place the year within commas, as if it were parenthetical. Do the same with the state or country in an address:

On March 3, *1970,* I was born in Kokomo, *Indiana,* during a blizzard.

NOTE: Do not use a comma between the state and the zip code.

E. To Group Words to Prevent Misreading

Inside, the dog was growling. [not *Inside the dog . . .*]
After eating, the child became sleepy. [not *After eating the child . . .*]

3. Do *Not* Use a Comma

A. To Separate Subject and Verb or Verb and Complement

Wrong: Deciduous *trees, change* color in the fall.
Right: Deciduous *trees change* color in the fall.

Wrong: On our trip we *saw,* countless *lakes* and *hills.*
Right: On our trip we *saw* countless *lakes* and *hills.*

B. **To Join Two Independent Clauses in Place of a Coordinate Conjunction** *(and, but, or, nor, for, yet, so)* **or Semicolon.** Avoiding this error, called a **comma splice**, is explained in G-10.2B, page 34.

P-2. The Period [.]

---

1. Use a Period

A. After Every Sentence Except a Direct Question or an Exclamation

The index dropped six points. [declarative sentence]
Sell your stocks now. [imperative sentence]
I asked how I should sell them. [indirect question; the direct question would be *How shall I sell them?*]

B. After an Abbreviation or Initial

Mr., U.S., Dr., Calif., M.D., Rev., lb.

NOTE: Ms. takes a period. *Miss* does not.

Do *not* use a period with

- Well-known initials of many organizations: IBM, FBI, CBS, UN, YMCA
- Radio and television stations: WSQK
- Money in even-dollar denominations: $40 (but $40.99)
- Contractions: ass'n, sec'y [for *association, secretary.* They may also be written *assn., secy.*]
- Ordinal numbers: 5th, 2nd, Henry VIII
- Nicknames: Rob, Pat, Sid, Pam
- Common shortened terms: memo, math, exam, lab, gym, TV [All these terms are colloquial; use the full words in formal writing.]

C. After a Number or Letter in a Formal Outline

   I.   Sports taught this semester
      A.   Swimming
      B.   Softball

NOTE: Do *not* use a period

- If the number or letter is within parentheses: (1), (a)
- If the number is part of a title: chapter 4, Henry V

See B-2, page 95, for more on outline form.

D. In a Group of Three (. . .) to Show

(1) *Ellipsis* (the intentional omission of words) in a quoted passage. Retain necessary punctuation preceding the ellipsis:

"But, in a larger sense, we cannot dedicate . . . this ground. The brave men, living and dead, . . . have consecrated it. . . ."

—Abraham Lincoln, "Gettysburg Address"

The first of the four final periods signals the end of the sentence.

(2) *Pause, hesitation, and the like* in dialogue and interrupted narrative (do not overuse this device):

"Perhaps I'm not fitted to be a mother? Perhaps . . . and if so . . . and how . . . ?"

—Doris Lessing, "A Man and Two Women"

E. After a Nonsentence. (A **nonsentence** is a legitimate unit of expression lacking subject + predicate. It is found mostly in dialog.)

(1) *A greeting:* Good morning.

(2) *A mild exclamation* not within a sentence:

Oh. Shucks.

(3) *An answer to a question:*

When can I get there? *By nine.*

NOTE: A nonsentence is a correct expression. A fragment (a similar structure *un*intentionally lacking subject + predicate) is an error. Fragments are explained in G-10.2A, page 34.

2. Do *Not* Use a Period After a Title of a composition or report, even if that title is a sentence:

Acid Rain in the 1990's
Acid Rain Is a Global Problem

Do, however, use a question mark or exclamation point where appropriate: *Acid Rain: Can We Stop It?*

P-3.　The Question Mark [?]

---

1. Use a Question Mark
A. After a Direct Question

Are you going? Where? At what time?
It's a long trip, isn't it?
You said—did I hear you correctly?—that you're ready.
You met her at the airport? [A question may be in declarative-sentence form; the question mark signals the tone in which it would be spoken.]

For use of the question mark in quotations, see P-8.3C, page 53; in titles, see P-2.2, above.

B. Within Parentheses to Indicate Doubt or Uncertainty
Chaucer was born in 1340(**?**) and died in 1400.

2. Do *Not* Use a Question Mark
A. After an Indirect Question
Sherwood asked whether I would be there.

B. After a Polite Request in Question Form
Will you kindly send me a copy of the report.

C. Within Parentheses to Express Humor or Irony
Wrong: They are such a charming (?) couple.

P-4.   The Exclamation Point [!]

---

1. Use an Exclamation Point After an Emphatic Word, Sentence, or Other Expression.

Wonderful!   I can't believe it!
Holy cow!   What a play!

For use of the exclamation point in titles, see P-2.2, page 45.

2. Do *Not* Use an Exclamation Point
A. After a Mild Interjection or a Sentence That Suggests Only Mild Excitement or Emotion. The exclamation point is a strong signal, but one that quickly loses its effect if overused. In general, outside of quoted dialog, reserve the exclamation point for expressions that begin with *how* or *what* (and are not questions). Elsewhere, use the less dramatic comma or period:

How crude of him!
Why, I never knew that.

B. More Than Once, or with Other Pause or Stop Marks
Wrong: Holy cow!!! [One ! is sufficient.]
Wrong: You sold the cow for a handful of beans?! [Use either ? or !]

For use of the exclamation point in quotations, see P-8.3C, page 53.

P-5.   The Semicolon [;]

The semicolon signals a greater break in thought than the comma but a lesser break than the period. It is, however, closer to a period than to a comma in most of its uses and is often interchangeable with the period. The semicolon often gives your writing a formal tone, as the following examples suggest.

Use a Semicolon

A. Between Independent Clauses Not Joined by a Coordinate Conjunction

Since the mid-1970's America's campuses have been relatively quiet; today's students seem interested more in courses than causes.

The semicolon is particularly effective for showing balance or contrast between two clauses:

The lakes abound with fish; the woods teem with game.

People are usually willing to give advice; they are much less inclined to take it.

B. Between Independent Clauses Joined by a Conjunctive Adverb

(*therefore, however, nevertheless, thus, moreover, also, besides, consequently, meanwhile, otherwise, then, also, furthermore, likewise, in fact, still*):

On weekdays we close at eleven; *however,* on weekends we stay open until one.

Take six courses this semester; *otherwise* you may not graduate.

NOTE: The comma after some conjunctive adverbs is optional.

Some conjunctive adverbs may drift into the second clause, but the semicolon remains between the clauses:

On weekdays we close at eleven; on weekends, *however,* we stay open until one.

C. Between Independent Clauses Joined by a Coordinate Conjunction When There Are Commas Within the Clauses

Today people can buy what they need from department stores, supermarkets, and discount stores; *but* in Colonial days, when such conveniences did not exist, people depended on general stores and peddlers. [The semicolon marks the break between the independent clauses more clearly than a comma would.]

D. Between Items in a Series When There Are Commas Within the Items

At the high school alumni dinner I sat with the school's best-known graduate, Harper Wyckoff; the editor of the school paper; two stars of the school play, a fellow and a girl who later married each other; and Tad Frump, the class clown.

P-6. The Apostrophe [']

1. Use an Apostrophe

A. To Form the Possessive Case of Nouns. A noun is possessive if it can also be expressed as the last word in an *of* phrase: the *captain's* chair = the chair *of the captain.*

(1) *Form the possessives of these with an apostrophe + s:*
   • *Almost all singular nouns:a woman's* coat
   Mr. Smith's car
   Ms. Davis's boat
   a bird's nest
   a person's legal right
   a fox's bushy tail
   the class's performance
   Lois's dingy old car

   • Plural nouns that
   do not end in *s:*
   the women's coats
   the people's legal rights
   the mice's nest

NOTE: Some authorities favor adding only an apostrophe to singular nouns ending in *s: Ms. Davis'*, *class'*. Whichever system you follow, be consistent.

(2) *Form the possessives of these with an apostrophe alone:*
   • *Plural nouns ending in s:*
   the Smiths' car
   two girls' coats
   the Davises' boat
   the birds' nests
   the boys' gymnasium
   the foxes' bushy tails
   the classes' performance

   • A few singular nouns
   that would sound awkward
   with another *s:*
   Ulysses' travels
   Sophocles' irony

CAUTION: Do not confuse the ordinary plural of nouns with the possessive. Ordinary plural: I know the *Smiths.* Possessive plural: The *Smiths'* cat died.

(3) *Use possessives before gerunds (verbal nouns).* Just as you say *I appreciated Jan's letter*, say *I appreciated **Jan's writing** so soon.* Other examples:

All were enchanted with the **professor's reminiscing.**

The **guests' singing** in the hallways upset the landlord.

See also G-6.2D(2), page 22.

(4) *Note these fine points of possession:*
  • Joint vs. individual possession: If two or more nouns possess something jointly, only the last noun gets an apostrophe:

Burglars ransacked *Marge and Ed's* apartment.

If each noun possesses a separate thing, each noun gets an apostrophe:

Burglars ransacked both *Donna's and Kathy's* apartments.

  • In hyphenated words, add the apostrophe to the last word only:

My *father-in-law's* remarriage has upset my wife.

  • Though possessive personal and interrogative pronouns do *not* take apostrophes (*yours, hers, whose,* etc.), possessive indefinite pronouns do: *anybody's, someone's, each other's, someone else's, everybody else's,* etc.
  • Words expressing time or amount usually form their possessive just as other nouns do: a *dollar's* worth, a *moment's* rest, a *week's* pay, two *weeks'* pay.

B. To Show Contractions and Other Omissions of Letters or Numerals

don't [do not]
who's [who is]
class of '92 [1992]
goin' [going]

C. For Clarity, to Form the Plurals of Letters, Numbers, Symbols, and Words Referred to as Words

Try not to use so many *and's.*
Last term she earned straight *A's.*
His *3's* and *5's* look too much alike.
Use *+'s* and *−'s* on the test.
Lola's career waned during the *1980's* [or 1980*s*].

2. Do *Not* Use an Apostrophe

A. With Possessive Personal Pronouns (*His, Hers, Its, Ours, Yours, Theirs*) or with *Whose*

Whose play caused the team's loss in *its* final game?
It was not *hers* or *yours;* it was *ours.* [See G-6.2D(3), page 22, and U, page 84., for *its/it's,* etc.]

B. To Form the Possessives of Inanimate Objects (unless the phrase using *of* sounds awkward):

Poor: the *house's* door
Better: the door *of the house*

But
Poor: the wait *of an hour*
Better: an *hour's* wait

C. To Form the Plurals of Proper Nouns

Merry Christmas from the *Altermatts*. [not *Altermatt's*]

P-7.   Italics (Underlining)

Italic type, or *italics,* is slanted type, as in the first words of this sentence. In your typing or handwriting, indicate italics by underlining: Moby Dick, *Moby Dick* .

Use Italics to Designate

A. Titles of Separate Publications

(1) *Books: The Tenants of Time* is a recent novel.

(2) *Magazines and newspapers:* Mr. Stanley reads the *New Yorker* and the *New York Times.*

   NOTE: The word *the* is not capitalized or italicized in a newspaper or magazine title.

(3) *Bulletins and pamphlets: Bee Production*

(4) *Plays, films, TV and radio programs, and musical productions:*

   Miller's *A View from the Bridge* [play]
   The Color Purple [film]
   Masterpiece Theater [television program]
   The Phantom of the Opera [musical production]

(5) *Poems long enough to be published separately:* Tennyson's *In Memoriam*

NOTE: Do not underline (or put within quotation marks) the title at the beginning of a composition or research paper unless the title contains words that would be underlined anyway, such as the title of a novel:

   A Birdwatcher's Paradise
   Symbolism in Steinbeck's *East of Eden*

B. Names of Ships, Aircraft, and Spacecraft

Schultz sailed on the *Nimitz.*
The spacecraft *Columbia* landed without incident.

C. Titles of Paintings and Sculptures

   The Blue Boy   *The Thinker*   *Mona Lisa*

NOTE: Some publications, especially some magazines and newspapers, use quotation marks or capitals instead of italics in many of the above

D. Foreign Words Not Yet Anglicized

It was a *fait accompli.*

NOTE: Consult your dictionary to find whether a word of foreign origin is considered a part of the English language, to be written without italics. Do not underline the common abbreviations *A.M., P.M., A.D., viz., vs., i.e., e.g., etc.*

E. Words, Letters, Figures, or Symbols Referred to as Such

The *t* in *often* is silent.
Avoid using *&* for *and* in formal writing.
Claude's *4*'s and *7*'s are indistinct.
Hester earned two *A*'s and three *B*'s.

F. Emphasis, where you cannot convey it by the order or choice of your words:

"You are *so* right," Fenwick remarked. [Only italics will convey the speaker's oral emphasis.]
I said that she *was* a good player. [The emphasis on *was* stresses that she no longer is.]

NOTE: Overuse of italics for emphasis is counterproductive because the italicized words no longer stand out sufficiently. Avoid such overuse.

P-8. Quotation Marks [" "]

Quotation marks enclose the exact words of a speaker, certain titles, or words used in a special sense. With one small exception, they are always used in *pairs.*

1. Use Regular (Double) Quotation Marks to Enclose

A. Direct Quotations (a speaker's exact words). Note that commas set off each quotation:

MacArthur vowed, "I shall return," as he left the islands.

NOTE: Do not use quotation marks with an *indirect* quotation (a paraphrase or summary of a speaker's words):

MacArthur vowed that he would return.

Observe these fine points of quotation-mark use.

(1) *With an interrupted quotation, use quotation marks around only the quoted words:*

"I heard," said Amy, "that you passed."

(2) *With an **un**interrupted quotation of several sentences, use quotation marks only before the first sentence and after the last:*

Wrong: Jenkins said, "Something's wrong." "I know it." "She should have called by now."
Right: Jenkins said, "Something's wrong. I know it. She should have called by now."

(3) *With an **un**interrupted quotation of several paragraphs, use either of the following forms:*
• Put quotation marks at the beginning of *each* paragraph but at the end of only the *last* paragraph.
• Use no quotation marks at all; instead, type the entire quotation as an indented block.

(4) *With a short quotation that is not a complete sentence, use no commas:*

Barrie describes life as "a long lesson in humility."

(5) *Use three periods to show the omission of unimportant or irrelevant words from a quotation* (ellipsis—see P-2.1D, page 44):

"What a heavy burden is a name that has become . . . famous."
—Voltaire

(6) *To insert your explanatory words into a quotation, use brackets (not parentheses).* See P-12, page 56.

(7) *When quoting dialog, start a new paragraph with each change of speaker:*

"He's dead," Holmes announced.
"Are you sure?" the young lady asked, her face blanching.

(8) *Do not use quotation marks around sets of quoted lines of poetry.* Type them as an indented block:

Grow old along with me!
The best is yet to be,
The last of life, for which the first was made:
—R. Browning, "Rabbi Ben Ezra"

However, you may run a very short poetic quotation into your text, using quotation marks (with a slash marking each line break):

Tennyson shows us an aged Ulysses, ". . . an idle king,/By this still hearth, among these barren crags."

B. Titles of Short Written Works: Poems, Articles, Essays, Short Stories, Chapters, Songs

"Song of the Open Road" is a poem in Walt Whitman's *Leaves of Grass.*
Chapter 1 of *The Guns of August* is titled "A Funeral."
I still get misty-eyed when Loretta sings "Danny Boy."

C. Definitions of Words

The original meaning of *lady* was "kneader of bread."

D. Words Used in a Special Sense or for a Special Purpose

The operation by the . . . city's Department of Investigation used apartments and hotel rooms specially "salted" with money and jewelry and monitored by video cameras.

—New York Times

NOTE: Occasionally you will see a slang expression or nickname enclosed in quotation marks, indicating that the writer recognizes the expression to be inappropriately informal. Avoid this apologetic use of quotation marks.

2. Use Single Quotation Marks [' '] to Enclose a Quotation Within a Quotation

Think of this construction as a box within a box. Ordinary double quotation marks [" "] provide the wrapping around the outer box; single quotation marks [' '] provide the wrapping around the inner box. Be sure to place end punctuation within the right box:

She asked, | "Who said, 'Let them eat cake' ?" |

3. Use Other Marks with Quotation Marks as Follows:

A. Periods and Commas.
Always put these marks *inside* closing quotation marks:

"I see it," whispered Watson. "It's the speckled band."

B. Colons and Semicolons.
Always put these marks *outside* closing quotation marks:

Coe barked, "I have nothing to say"; then he left.
Three students selected "Endymion": Burke, Rizzo, and Stecz.

C. Question Marks, Exclamation Points, and Dashes.
Place these marks *inside* the quotation marks when they belong to the quotation, *outside* otherwise:

Shauna asked, "Who is my opponent?" [The quotation is the question.]
Did Shauna say, "I fear no opponent"? [The part outside the quotation is the question.]
Did Shauna say, "Who is my opponent"? [Both the quotation and the outside part are questions. Use only one question mark—the outside one.]
"I don't believe it!" she exclaimed.

How furious he was when she muttered, "I don't know"!
"How could you do—" Cressida began, but faltered.
"Here"—Holmes threw open the door—"is our culprit!"

4. Do *Not* Use Quotation Marks

A. To Enclose the Title Introducing a Composition or Research Paper (unless the title is a quotation):

Wrong: "Overproduction as a Cause of the Depression"
Right: Overproduction as a Cause of the Depression

B. To Show That a Word Is Intended Ironically or Humorously.
Your irony or humor will be more effective if not so blatantly pointed out:

Wrong: The way she "keeps house" is not to be believed.
Right: The way she keeps house is not to be believed.

P-9. The Colon [:]

---

1. Use a Colon to Introduce

A. A List That Follows a Grammatically Complete Statement. The list is usually in apposition to some word in the statement:

Our backfield consists of four rookies: Tucker, Galgano, Smyth, and Mack. [The four names are in apposition to *rookies*.]
We hired Ms. Roe for one reason: her experience. [*Experience* is a one-item "list" in apposition to *reason*.]
Her choices were these: to say nothing, to file a grievance, or to resign. [The three choices are in apposition to *these*.]

Often *the following* or *as follows* precedes the colon:

To the mixture, add one or more of *the following:* nutmeg, thyme, basil, parsley, or cloves.

Do *not* use a colon if an *in*complete statement precedes the list (verb without complement, preposition without object, etc.):

Our backfield consists of Tucker, Galgano, Smyth, and Mack.
We hired Mrs. Roe for her experience.
Her choices were to say nothing, to file a grievance, or to resign.

B. A Long Quotation (one or more paragraphs):

In *The Art of the Novel* Henry James wrote:

The house of fiction has in short not one window, but a million—a number of possible windows not to be reckoned, rather. . . . [quotation continues for one or more paragraphs]

C. A Formal Quotation or Question

The President declared: "The only thing we have to fear is fear itself."

The question is: What can we do? [or *The question is: what can we do?*]

D. A Second Independent Clause That Explains the First Clause

Potter's motive is clear: he wants the inheritance.

E. The Body of a Business Letter (after the greeting):

Dear Sir: Dear Ms. Weiner:

NOTE: Use a comma after the greeting of a personal (friendly) letter.

F. The Details Following an Announcement

For sale: mountain cabin

G. A Formal Resolution, After the Word *Resolved*

Resolved: That this council petition the mayor to . . .

H. The Words of a Speaker in a Play (after the speaker's name):

Macbeth: She should have died hereafter.

2. Use a Colon to Separate

A. Parts of a Title, Reference, or Numeral

Title: *Principles of Mathematics: An Introduction*
Reference: Luke 3: 4–13
Numeral: 8:15 P.M.

B. The Place of Publication from the Publisher, and the Volume Number from the Pages, in Bibliographies

Seagrave, Sterling. *The Marcos Dynasty.* New York: Harper, 1988.
Jarchow, Elaine. "In Search of Consistency in Composition Scoring."
English Record 23.4 (1982): 18–19.

P-10. The Dash [—]

The dash is a dramatic mark, signaling an abrupt break in the flow of a sentence. Do not use it for an ordinary pause or stop in place of a comma, period, or semicolon. On a typewriter, make a dash by using two strokes of the hyphen key, with no spaces before, between, or after--like this.

Use a Dash

A. To Show a Sudden Break in Thought

I'll give—let's see, what can I give?
Well, if that's how you feel—
Quisenberry began, "May I ask—?"

B. To Set Off a Parenthetical Element that is long, that sharply interrupts the sentence, or that otherwise would be hard to distinguish:

The train arrived—can you believe it?—right on time.
We traveled by foot, in horse-drawn wagons, and occasionally—if we had some spare cash, if the farmers felt sorry for us, or if we could render some service in exchange—atop a motorized tractor.

C. To Emphasize an Appositive

He had only one interest—food. [or . . . *interest: food.*]
Drill, inspections, calisthenics—all are part of army life.
The basic skills—reading, writing, and mathematics—are stressed here.

NOTE: The colon also emphasizes but imparts a more formal tone than the dash.

D. To Precede the Author's Name After a Direct Quotation

"Short words are best and the old words when short are best of all."
—Winston Churchill

P-11.   Parentheses [( )]

---

1. Use Parentheses (Always in Pairs)
A. To Set Off Incidental Information or Comment

Senator Rollins (R., Iowa) chairs the committee.
The painting (probably the most original in the exhibition) at first occasioned little notice.

NOTE: Do not overuse parentheses. Use commas to set off ordinary parenthetical (interrupting) expressions. Do not use an opening capital letter or closing period with a sentence in parentheses within a larger sentence.

B. To Enclose

(1) *Letters or figures in enumeration:*

She is authorized to (1) sign checks, (2) pay bills, and (3) make purchases.

(2) *References and directions:*

The map (see page 70) will help you.

(3) *A question mark indicating uncertainty:*

He was born in 1897(?) in Boise, Idaho.

C. For Accuracy, in Legal Documents and Business Letters

I enclose fifty dollars ($50).

D. With Other Punctuation Marks as Follows

(1) *The comma, semicolon, and period* follow the closing parenthesis when the parentheses set off material in a sentence:

If we go **(**we are still not sure**),** you too may go.
He deceived us **(**weren't we foolish**?);** he was clever.
I believed her **(**though I can't imagine why**).**

(2) *The question mark and the exclamation point* go inside the parentheses if the mark belongs to the parenthetical element; otherwise, they go outside:

One of the translators was Aquila **(**died A.D. 138**?).**
Have you read the translation of Tyndale **(**died 1536**)?**
Snerd asked my fiancée for a date **(**what gall**!).**

2. Do *Not* Use Parentheses

A. To Indicate Deletions. Instead draw a line through the deleted words:

Wrong: (Never) Seldom have I seen such gall.
Right: ~~Never~~ Seldom have I seen such gall.

B. To Enclose Editorial Comment. Use brackets for this purpose, as explained in the next section.

P-12.   Brackets [   ]

Use Brackets

A. To Enclose Your Editorial or Explanatory Remarks Within a Direct Quotation

Churchill said in 1940, "If we can stand up to him [Hitler], all Europe may be free. . . ."

B. With *Sic* to Mark the Original Writer's Error in Material You Are Quoting

The note ended, "Respectively [sic] yours, Martha."

NOTE: Sic is Latin for "Thus it is." Its use clarifies that the error was made not by you but by the person you are quoting.

C. To Enclose Stage Directions

MIRANDA [*sipping her coffee*]: Are you glad to see me?

P-13.   The Hyphen [-]

Use a Hyphen

A. To Join Certain Compound Words (consult a dictionary to ascertain which):

mother-in-law   go-getter   jack-o'-lantern

B. To Join Words Used as a Single Adjective Before a Noun

Route 303 is a *well-paved* road.
She tried *door-to-door* selling.

NOTE: Do not hyphenate such a modifier when it *follows* a noun as a subject complement: Route 303 is *well paved.* Do not use a hyphen between an *-ly* adverb and an adjective: *freshly baked* bread.

C. When Writing Out Two-Word Numbers from 21 to 99 and Two-Word Fractions

twenty-two   three-fourths
fifty-first   five twenty-fourths
two hundred ten   two hundred twenty-two

Also hyphenate a compound adjective containing a number:

ten-year-old boy   forty-hour week   hundred-yard dash
ten-dollar bill   two- and three-room apartments

D. To Avoid Ambiguity

Ambiguous: The advertisement was intended for *old train buffs.* [*old buffs of trains* or *buffs of old trains?*]
Clear: The advertisement was intended for *old-train buffs.*

E. With the Prefixes *ex-* (When It Means "former"), *self-, all-,* and the Suffix *-elect*

ex-president   self-confidence
all-conference   Senator-elect Doe

NOTE: The modern tendency is to join nearly all prefixes and suffixes to root words without hyphens, except where ambiguity (*recover, re-cover*) or awkwardness might result or where the root is capitalized (*anti-American, Europe-wide*). Examples of modern usage are *antiterrorist, noninterventionist, semiliterate* (but *semi-independent,* to avoid an awkward double *i*), *bimonthly, triweekly, citywide.*

F. To Indicate Words That Are Spelled Out and Hesitation or Stuttering

"She wants a d-o-l-l," her mother said.
"I'm f-f-frightened," he stammered.

G. To Divide a Word That Will Not Fit at the End of a Line

The classroom can accom-
modate thirty students.

NOTE: Always put the hyphen at the end of the first line, not at the beginning of the second line. Do not guess where a word should divide; consult your dictionary. See M-3, page 64, for more details on syllabication.

MECHANICS

The term *mechanics* is usually understood to include spelling and punctuation, but each of these is important and complex enough to warrant its own section in this book. This section treats the remaining points of mechanics—the technical conventions that apply only to the written form of our language. Correct mechanics in your paper signals that you are a careful writer, taking pains to make your reader's task easier.

M-1. Manuscript Form

1. Handwritten Papers. Use lined white paper 8½ by 11 inches. Write on one side of the paper only, unless your instructor permits otherwise. Do not use paper torn from notebooks. Write on alternate lines unless lines are at least three-eighths of an inch apart. Use black or blue ink. Write legibly; a word difficult to decipher may be marked as an error. Clearly distinguish between capital and lowercase letters.

2. Typed Papers. Use unlined white bond paper of good quality, 8½ by 11 inches. Type on one side of the paper only. Do not use colored paper or paper that lets type show through. Use a black ribbon; change it before it gets pale. Keep the keys clean.

Use double spacing. Follow standard conventions in typing. If your typewriter does not have a figure *1,* use the lowercase l, not capital I. Check your paper for typing mistakes; they may be counted as errors if uncorrected.

3. Papers Done on Word Processors. Be sure that the print is dark and that the paper is of high quality. Set a dot-matrix printer for near-letter-quality (NLQ) printing if available. Adjust the paper in the printer to give adequate top and bottom margins. Turn on pagination if available. Neatly separate fanfold pages and remove side guide strips.

4. Spacing. Leave margins of 1 inch for the top and sides of each page, and either 1 or 1½ inches at the bottom.

Indent 1 inch for paragraphs in handwritten papers; indent five spaces in typewritten papers. Do *not* indent the first line of a page unless it begins a new paragraph. Do not crowd lines at the bottom of a page; use another sheet even though it will contain only a line or two.

Separate from the text any prose quotations longer than *four lines* or verse quotations of *two or more lines;* use no quotation marks, use double spacing, and indent ten spaces from the left (1 inch in a handwritten paper). Keep shorter prose quotations in the body of the text and enclose them in quotation marks.

5. Title.
Center the title on the first line of page 1. Leave the next line blank, and begin writing on the third line. See P-2.2, page 45; P-8.4A, page 53; and M-2.1F, page 61, for punctuation and capitalization of titles. Do not repeat the title after page 1.

6. Page Numbers.
Number all pages, after the first, with Arabic numerals (*2, 3, 4,* etc.) in the upper right-hand corner. Use no periods or parentheses with the numbers.

7. Proofreading.
Before handing in a paper, read it thoroughly for errors in spelling, punctuation, wording, and sentence construction. If you have many errors, redo the page or even the whole paper, especially if you are word-processing. If not redoing, make changes as follows:

A. Deletion of One or More Words. Draw a horizontal line through words to be deleted: Return ~~back~~ here tomorrow. (Do not use parentheses.)

B. Deleting of Spaces. Draw sideways parentheses (⌒) around the space to be deleted:

w‿ord

C. Insertion of One or More Words. Write words to be inserted above the line and use a caret (∧) to show point of insertion:

only he could ∧ known *have*

D. Insertion of Space. Use a caret (∧) to indicate insertion and a pound mark (#) to indicate space:

aspace. #

Or, draw a slash between the two words: a/space.

E. Transposed Letters. Use a sideways S (∽) around the letters to show that they should occur in the opposite order:

lett(r/e)s

F. Capital Letters. To indicate that a lower case letter should be capitalized, draw three lines under it:

american.

G. Lower-case Letters. Draw a slash (/) through a capital letter that should be a lower-case letter:

ℓetter.

H. Paragraphing. Use the ¶ sign to show the point at which you wish to indicate a new paragraph. Write *No* ¶ if you wish to remove a paragraph indention.

M-2. Capitalization

---

1. Use Capital Letters for

A. The First Word of Every Sentence. This includes quoted sentences:

She said, "The work is finished."

Do *not* capitalize the first word of

- An indirect quotation (paraphrase): She said *that the work was finished.*
- A fragmentary quotation: She said that the work was "almost finished."
- A sentence in parentheses within another sentence: She said (did I tell you?) that the work was finished.

B. The First Word of a Line of Poetry (unless the poet has used lowercase):

Had we but world enough, and time,
This coyness, lady, were no crime.
— Andrew Marvell, "To His Coy Mistress"

C. Words and Phrases Used as Sentences

Why?   Certainly.   Yes, indeed.   Of course.

D. The First Word of a Formal Question or Statement Following a Colon

He asked several questions: Where are you going? What will you do? Where is your goal?
I offer a word of advice: Read only the best books.

E. The First Word of Each Item in a Formal Outline

I. Sports taught this semester
   A. Swimming
   B. Softball

F. Important Words in a Title

Across the River and into the Trees [book]
"A Horse Foaled by an Acorn" [chapter]

Always capitalize the first and the last word. Capitalize all other words *except*

(1) *Articles* (a, an, *and* the):
   Closing the Ring

(2) *Prepositions* (on, in, to . . .):
   The Winds of War

(3) to *in an infinitive:*
   How to Take Good Pictures

(4) *Coordinate conjunctions* (and, but . . .):
   The Power and the Glory

NOTE: Some authorities favor capitalizing prepositions of five or more letters, such as *about: Much Ado About Nothing.* Most authorities favor not capitalizing *the* beginning a newspaper or magazine title: I read the *New Yorker.*

Always capitalize the first word following a dash or colon:
   F. Scott Fitzgerald: A Study of the Stories.

G. The First and Last Words in the Salutation (Greeting) of a Letter and the First Word in the Complimentary Close

My dearest Son,   Very truly yours,

H. Proper Nouns and Adjectives Made from Them. A proper noun, as distinguished from a common noun, is the name of a specific person, place, or thing. A proper adjective is made from a proper noun: *America, American; Shakespeare, Shakespearean:*

Proper Noun	*Common Noun*
Stella	woman
New Orleans	city
July	month
York College	college
Chamber of Commerce	organization

(1) *Specific persons, races, tribes, nationalities, and languages:*

Louisa May Alcott	Inuit	Caucasian
Italian	Japanese	Latin

NOTE: It is not customary to capitalize *black, white, aborigine,* and similar racial descriptions.

(2) *Specific places* (countries, states, cities, geographic sections; oceans, lakes, rivers; streets, buildings, rooms, parks, monuments, etc.):

Japan	Atlantic Ocean	State Street
Iowa	Lake Algonquin	the Todd Building
Springfield	Missouri River	Room 164
the Far East	Fairmont Park	Lincoln Memorial

(3) *Specific organizations:*

the Giants	Knights of Columbus	United Nations
Red Cross	Ace Tire Company	

(4) *Days of the week, months, and holidays:*

Friday	August	Fourth of July	Labor Day

(5) *Religious names considered sacred:*

God	Heavenly Father	Yahweh
the Virgin	the Christ Child	Allah
the Lord	the Most High	the Savior

NOTE: The modern tendency is not to capitalize pronouns referring to the Deity except to avoid ambiguity: *Trust in* **H**im. But *May God shed* **h**is *grace on you.*

(6) *Historical events, periods, and documents:*

Battle of the Bulge	the Civil Rights Act
the Renaissance	Magna Charta

(7) *Names of educational institutions, departments, courses, classes of students, and specific academic degrees:*

Washboard College	Biology 101 (but see
Junior Class	2D below)
Sc.D. (Doctor of Science)	Department of Philosophy

(8) *Names of flags, emblems, and school colors:*

the Stars and Stripes	Bronze Star	the Blue and Gold

(9) *Stars and planets:*

the North Star	Mars	the Big Dipper

NOTE: Do not capitalize *sun* and *moon* unless they are personified (considered as persons). Do not capitalize *earth* unless it is personified or considered as one of the planets.

(10) *Ships, trains, aircraft, and spacecraft:*

Titanic	*Spirit of St. Louis*	*Columbia*

(11) *Initials* indicating time, divisions of the government, telephone exchanges, call letters of radio and TV stations; and certain other well-known sets of initials:

B.C.	TV	PE 6-5000
FBI	IBM	O.K. (or OK)
WABX	A.M.	NASA

(12) *Personifications:*

Mother Nature	Old Man Winter	the eye of Death

(13) *A title preceding a name:*

Professor Jane Melton   Chief Justice Marshall
General Eisenhower   the Reverend Beliveau

Do not capitalize a title following a name unless the title shows very high national or international distinction:

Jane Melton, professor of history
George Bush, President of the United States

You may capitalize a title of very high distinction when used instead of the person's name. Be consistent in this usage:

The President addressed Congress.

Capitalize an abbreviated title before or after a name:

Prof. Susan Zulli, Ph.D.   Sen. Robert Clark, Jr.

I. The Pronoun *I* and the Interjection *O*

May I always worship thee, O Zeus.

NOTE: Do not capitalize *oh* unless some other rule applies.

2. Do *Not* Capitalize

A. Points of the Compass (unless they refer to a specific geographic locality):

She flew east from Denver, not north.
Her family lived in the Middle West.
Russia and the West are holding arms talks.

B. Seasons (unless personified):
Paul goes south every winter.

"Gentle Spring! in sunshine clad . . ."
—Charles D'Orleans, "Spring"

C. Words Denoting a Family Relationship, when they follow a possessive noun or pronoun:

She is Charlie's aunt.
I wrote to my mother.

But do capitalize when the family relationship is used as a title preceding a name or by itself as if a name:

Here comes Uncle Sid.   I love you, Father.

D. Names of Academic Disciplines (unless they are part of specific course titles or proper nouns):

I could never pass mathematics or physics.
I passed Differential Calculus II. [specific course title]
I majored in English and French. [proper nouns]

E. Common Nouns (unless they are part of proper nouns):

I was a senior at the high school in our township.
At Hamilton High School in Tucker Township, I was president of the Senior Class.

F. The First Word After a Semicolon

Fay handed in her paper; then she left.

G. The First Word in the Latter Part of an Interrupted Quotation (unless that word begins a new sentence):

"My goal," said Jo, "is to skydive." [one quoted sentence]
"I have one goal," said Jo. "It is to skydive." [*It* begins a new quoted sentence.]

H. The First Word of a Quotation That Is Not a Complete Sentence

She described him as a "bright and serious student."

I. The Second Part of Most Compound Words (but capitalize when that part is a proper noun):

Forty-second Street   all-American

J. A Word That You Want to Emphasize (use italics instead):

Wrong: The label said NOT to shake.
Right: The label said *not* to shake.

M-3. Syllabication

Sometimes you must break a word at the end of a line. Avoid doing so whenever possible; especially avoid breaking two successive lines. When breaking a word is unavoidable, mark the division with a hyphen (made with one stroke on the typewriter [-]). A good dictionary is your most reliable guide to the hyphenation of words. Remembering the following general rules, however, will reduce your need to consult the dictionary.

1. Divide According to Pronunciation; Always Divide Between Syllables.
Leave enough of a word at the end of the first line to suggest the sound and meaning of the whole word: *com-plete, monot-onous, change-able.*

2. Divide Compound Words Between the Parts:
hand-book, book-keeper, rattle-snake. If a compound word is already hyphenated, break it at an existing hyphen: *sister-in-law, self-portrait.*

3. Do Not Divide a One-Syllable Word of Any Length:
straight, through, dropped, slipped, found.

4. Do Not Set Off a Single Letter as a Syllable.

Wrong: a-way   scar-y
Right: away   scary

M-4. Numbers

1. Generally, Write Out a Number in Words When

A. It Will Take Only One or Two Words: *forty* bushels, *thirty-nine* steps, *two hundred* spectators, *thirty-third* floor.

B. The Number Is Part of a Compound Adjective: an *eight-hour* day, a *five-year-old* girl, a *six-room* house.

C. The Number Is a Fraction Unaccompanied by a Whole Number: *one-fourth* of your pay, *two-fifths* of a mile.

NOTE: Use figures otherwise: The house is *4½* miles from Rome.

D. The Number Begins a Sentence

Three hundred fifty copies were all that the book sold.

Never begin a sentence with a figure. If the number is a long one, rewrite the sentence to place the number elsewhere:

The book sold only *2,876* copies.

2. Use Figures for

A. Any Number That Would Be Three or More Words When Written Out

This dormitory houses *138* students.

Use commas to separate every set of three digits (except in serial and telephone numbers, addresses, years in dates, and page numbers). Count from the right or the decimal point:

2,876 copies   *$1,345,009.59*
A.D. *1066*   *1456* East Drive

Write very large round numbers as follows:

two million   *23 million*   *4.2 trillion*

B. Dates; Addresses; Room Numbers; Telephone Numbers; Chapter, Page, and Line Numbers; Serial Numbers; Decimals and Percentages; Route Numbers; Times; Statistics; and Precise Measurements

March *20, 1931*	*117* Bly Road	Room *114*
224–8575	chapter *4*	*998-47-3373*
32.7	*7* percent	Route *6*
3:30 P.M.	*92* for; *37* against	*6* by *3.2* inches
		[but *six feet long*]

NOTE: Observe these cautions.

• Do not use *-st, -th,* etc. after figures in dates:
> Wrong: March *15th, 1992*
> Right: March *15, 1992* [but *the fifteenth of March*]

• In formal writing, do not use the form *3/20/92* for a date.

• In writing a time, use figures with A.M. and P.M. and when emphasizing an exact time. Generally, use words otherwise:
> *3* P.M.   from *2:30* to *3:00* A.M.   at *9:45* tomorrow
> *four* o'clock   around *half-past five*

C. Groups of Numbers in the Same Passage (do not mix words and figures):

> Vote totals by precinct were *135, 78, 10, 166,* and *23.*

3. Write Amounts of Money as Follows:

I earn *sixty-five dollars* a week.
I earn *$65.50* a week.
I earn *$310* a week.
I won *$40, $30,* and *$5* at the races.
She won *a million dollars.*
She won *$6 million.*
She won *$6,889,346.*

M-5.   Abbreviations

Abbreviations are intended mainly for limited spaces, such as signs, lists, and footnotes. In ordinary writing, avoid abbreviations except for those listed in 1 below.

1. In Ordinary Writing, Abbreviate

A. Certain Titles Before Proper Names: *Mr., Mrs., Ms., Dr., St.* (*saint*), *Messrs., Mmes.*

Write *Reverend* and *Honorable* in full if they follow *the:*

the Reverend Irwin Smyth   *the Honorable* Beatrice Bloom
Rev. Irwin Smyth   *Hon.* Beatrice Bloom

Write military and political titles in full if you use only the person's last name:
Major General Puffington   *Senator* Claghorn
Maj. Gen. John Puffington   *Sen.* Calpurnia Claghorn

B. Certain Titles, Including Degrees, After Proper Names: *Sr.* (*senior*), *Jr., Esq., M.A., Ph.D.:*

Eula B. Smith, *Ed.D.,* is the main speaker.
Rev. Joseph O'Hare, *S.J.,* presided.

C. Certain Expressions Used with Numerals: *A.M., P.M., A.D., B.C.,* No. (*number*), *$:*

9:30 *A.M.*   *A.D.* 1066
450 *B.C.*   *No.* 484
$43.50

Wrong: She arrived this *A.M.* [no numeral with *A.M.*]
Right: She arrived this *morning.*

D. Certain Latin Phrases: *i.e.* (*that is*), *viz.* (*namely*), *e.g.* (*for example*), *cf.* (*compare*), *etc.* (*and so forth*), *vs.* (*versus*).

NOTE: Publishers tend to discourage the use of these abbreviations in the text of formal writing; you would do better to write out the English equivalents unless space is restricted (as in notes). Never write *and etc.;* it is redundant. See U, page 81.

E. Certain Governmental Agencies and Other Well-Known Organizations: *FBI, NASA, NAACP, CBS, IBM.* To be sure that your reader knows the meaning of such initials, give the full title the first time:

Leaders of the *Central Intelligence Agency* met with the President. The *CIA* officials had no comment afterward.

2. In Ordinary Writing, Do *Not* Abbreviate

A. Names of States, Countries, Months, or Days

Wrong: He left for *N.J.* last *Fri.*
Right: He left for *New Jersey* last *Friday.*

B. Personal Names

Wrong: Is *Geo.* coming home?
Right: Is *George* coming home?

C. The Word *Christmas.* (Avoid *Xmas.*)

D. The Words *Street, Avenue, Road, Park,* and *Company,* especially as part of proper names:

Wrong: The Harding *Co.* is on Fifth *St.*
Right: The Harding *Company* is on Fifth *Street.*

E. The Word *and,* except in names of firms: *Ways and Means Committee; the Smith & Barnes Company.*

F. References to a School Subject

Wrong: The *phys. ed.* class was dismissed.
Right: The *physical education* class was dismissed.

G. The Words *Volume, Chapter,* and *Page* (except in footnotes, tabulations, and technical writing; see a good dictionary for other abbreviations used in such writing).

SPELLING

Misspelling is the gravy stain of writing. Misspelled words affect your reader the way a large glob of gravy on your best suit or dress would affect someone you were trying to impress. Because misspelling and incompetence are usually associated in a reader's mind, make every effort to purge faulty spelling habits from your writing. Consult a dictionary whenever you doubt the spelling of a word. Keep a list of words you frequently misspell (people tend to misspell the same words again and again), and try to analyze the reasons for your recurring errors. You can correct most of them by attention to one or more of the following suggestions.

S-1. Techniques for Spelling Improvement

1. Visualize the Correct Spelling of a Word. Look attentively at a word; then look away from it and try to see the printed word in your mind.

2. Practice Pronouncing and Spelling Troublesome Words Aloud, Syllable by Syllable.

ath-let-ic	quan-ti-ty
en-vi-ron-ment	ac-ci-den-tal-ly
gov-ern-ment	lab-or-a-to-ry

3. Practice Writing a Troublesome Word Several Times. Begin slowly and increase your speed until the right form comes easily. You will need drill to substitute correct spelling habits for faulty ones.

4. Distinguish Between Words Similar in Sound or Spelling. See U, pages 74–92, for explanations of the following and many other such distinctions:

to/too/two	lose/loose	its/it's	whose/who's
your/you're	there/their/they're	woman/women	

5. Do Not Drop, Add, or Change Letters When Adding Prefixes or Suffixes or Combining Roots unless you know that the word is irregular or that a spelling rule applies (see 6b-6e below; S-2, page 72; and U, pages 74–92):

Prefix + Root	*Root + Suffix*	*Root + Root*
dis/appear	careful/ly	book/keeper
dis/satisfied	immediate/ly	grand/daughter
mis/spell	comical/ly	
re/commend	state/ment	
im/moral		

6. Master These Spelling Rules.

A. The *ie-ei* Rule: This version of the old jingle should help:

When the sound is like *EE*,
Put *i* before *e*—
Except after *c*.

That is, when the sound of the two letters is *EE* (as in *see*), use *ie* (*chief, grief, niece, hygiene, field, relief*) unless a *c* precedes (*receive, conceit, ceiling, deceive*). When the sound is not *EE*, write *ei* (*eight, height, their, foreign, counterfeit, veil*).

Remember these odd sentences for the common exceptions:

ie: The finan**cier**'s spe**cie**s is fri**e**ndly.
ei: N**ei**ther w**ei**rd prot**ei**n s**ei**zes l**ei**sure.

NOTE: The *ie* jingle does not apply when the *i* and *e* are in separate syllables (*sci ence*).

B. The Final *e* Rule: Drop a final silent *e* before a suffix beginning with a vowel (*a, e, i, o, u,* and here *y*):

write + ing = writing	fame + ous = famous
love + able = lovable	scare + y = scary
hope + ed = hoped	come + ing = coming

Keep the *e* when the suffix does not begin with a vowel: *hope/ful, love/less, lone/ly, safe/ty, state/ment, same/ness.*

Keep the *e* before a vowel suffix

(1)   *After c and* g, to keep a "soft" sound before a suffix beginning with *a* or *o*: *notice/able, change/able, courage/ous.*

(2)   *To avoid confusion with other words: singe + ing = singe/ing* (to avoid confusion with *singing*); *dye + ing = dye/ing.*

C. The Final *y* Rule: Change a final *y* to *i* before any suffix except *-ing*:

happy + ness = happiness	cry + ed = cried
busy + ly = busily	lady + s = ladies

cry/ing   bury/ing   try/ing

Ignore this rule if a vowel precedes the *y*:

chimn**ey**/s   ann**oy**/ed   monk**ey**/s

Exceptions: lay, laid; pay, paid; say, said.

D. The Doubling Rule: Double a final consonant before a suffix beginning with a vowel (including *y*) if the original word

(1)   *ends in consonant-vowel-consonant (cvc)*

(2)   *and is accented on the last syllable (this includes all one-syllable words):*

   cvc   **cvc**   **cvc**
drop, drop/**p**ing; bat, bat/**t**er; hum, hum/**m**able

   cvc   **cvc**
occUR, occUR/**r**ed; conTROL, conTROL/**l**ing;

   cvc
reFER, reFER/**r**al

                                    vvc
Otherwise, do not double. Not *cvc: droop, droop/ing;*

vcc   **vvc**
milk, milk/ed; enTAIL, enTAIL/ing. Not accented on last syllable: *BENefit, BENefit/ed; OFfer, OFfer/ing.*

NOTE: If the accent shifts to an earlier syllable when the suffix is added, do not double: *conFER, CONfer/ence*

E. Rules for Forming Plurals: To form most plurals, add -*s* to the singular (*toy, toys; dollar, dollars*; *Donna Remington, the Remingtons*). The following generalizations cover most other plurals. Consult your dictionary in other cases or when in doubt.

(1)   *If you hear an added syllable when you say a plural, add* -es *when you write it: bush, bush/es; fox, fox/es; buzz, buzz/es; church, church/es.*

(2)   *Add* -es *when the final* y *rule applies (see C above): sky, skies; liberty, liberties.*

(3)   *With the following and a few other nouns, change the final* f *or* fe *to* v *and add* -es: *calf, calves; knife, knives; wife, wives; loaf, loaves; wharf, wharves; life, lives.*

(4)   *With certain singular nouns ending in* o, *add* -es: *tomato, tomatoes; potato, potatoes; hero, heroes.* With almost all other singular nouns ending in *o*, add just -*s*. (With musical terms, such as *solo, piano, alto*, and words ending in a vowel + *o*, such as *radio, studio*, always add just -*s*.) With a few final *o* words, you may use either -*s* or -*es*: *domino, dominos* or *dominoes; zero, zeros* or *zeroes.* Consult a dictionary for plurals of other final *o* words.

(5)   *Add the plural ending to the very end of solid (unhyphenated) compound words: cupfuls, spoonfuls.* Add it to the noun in hyphenated compounds: *fathers-in-law, passers-by.*

(6) *With certain nouns of foreign origin, use the foreign plural:*

alumnus, alumn*i*   alumna, alumn*ae*
stimulus, stimul*i*   crisis, cris*es*
oasis, oas*es*   hypothesis, hypothes*es*
partenthesis, parenthes*es*   thesis, thes*es*
analysis, analys*es*   axis, ax*es*
synopsis, synops*es*

NOTE: With many other such nouns, you may use either the foreign or English plural:

radius, radii or *radiuses*
stadium, stadi*a* or *stadiums*
octopus, octop*i* or *octopuses*
index, ind*ices* or *indexes*
appendix, append*ices* or *appendixes*
antenna, antenn*ae* (of insects) or *antennas* (of TV sets)
phenomenon, phenomena or *phenomenons*
criterion, criteri*a* or *criterions*
vertebra, vertebr*ae* or *vertebras.*

Many of these use the foreign plural in scholarly or technical writing and the English plural in general writing. Your dictionary may specify when each should be used.

(7) *With numbers, letters, and symbols, add -'s for clarity: a's; 6's, +'s, and's, 1990's* [or *1990s*].

7. Make Full Use of Memory Devices.
Associate one word with another, find a word within a word, or make up jingles or nonsense sentences; such **mnemonics** can help you over the trouble spots in your problem words:

Emma is in a dil*emma.*
She put a *dent* in the superinten*dent.*
Station*e*ry is pap*e*r.
A princip*le* is a ru*le.*
Poor gram*mar* will *mar* your writing.
It is *vile* to have no pri*vile*ges.
The *villa*in owns a *villa* in Spain.
There is *a rat* in sep*arat*e and in comp*arat*ive.
I have *lice* on my *lice*nse!
There is *iron* in the env*iron*ment.
There is a *meter* in the ce*meter*y.
Tim has great op*tim*ism.
With any pro*fes*sor, one *F* is enough.
An *engine* has plenty of str*engt*h.

Group words with similar characteristics, such as two sets of double letters (a*cc*o*mm*odate, e*mb*a*rr*ass, po*ss*e*ss*) or three *i*'s (*optimistic, primitive*) or names of occupations (auth*or*, cens*or*, conduct*or*, em-

*per**or**, invest**or**, spons**or**, profess**or***) or the three *-ceed* words (If you *pro**ceed*** to *ex**ceed***, you will *suc**ceed***. All other words ending in the same sound are spelled with *-cede*, except *super**sede***).

8. Proofread Your Completed Manuscript. Doing so will help you detect—and correct—all misspelled words. Use a dictionary when in doubt.

S-2.　180 Words Often Misspelled

(Sets of words that are often confused, such as *advice* and *advise*, are explained in U, pages 74–92.)

1. absence
   accidentally
   accommodate
   achievement
   acknowledge
   acquaintance
   acquire
   acquitted
   across
   adolescence

2. aggressive
   amateur
   analysis
   anxious
   apologize
   apparent
   approximately
   argument
   article
   athlete

3. auxiliary
   believe
   benefited
   business
   category
   cemetery
   changeable
   character
   committee
   comparatively

4. competent
   competition
   conceivable
   condemn
   conscientious
   conscious
   courteous
   criticism
   curiosity
   deceive

5. definite
   describe
   description
   desirable
   desperate
   develop
   disappear
   disappoint
   disastrous
   discipline

6. dilemma
   dissatisfied
   doesn't
   ecstasy
   eighth
   embarrass
   entirely
   environment
   erroneous
   etc.*

7. exaggerate
   excellent
   exhilaration
   existence
   familiar
   fascinating
   fictitious
   finally
   forcibly
   foreign

8. forfeit
   forty
   fulfill
   government
   grammar
   guarantee
   guidance
   height
   hindrance
   hoping

9. hypocrisy
   immediately
   incidentally
   independent
   indispensable
   intelligence
   irrelevant*
   irresistible
   kindergarten
   knowledge

*See also U, pages 74–92.

10. laboratory
    maintenance
    management
    maneuver
    mathematics
    meant
    millionaire
    mischievous
    misspelled
    necessary

11. niece
    ninety
    ninth
    noticeable
    nucleus
    occasionally
    occurred
    occurrence
    omission
    omitted

12. opinion
    opportunity
    optimistic
    outrageous
    parallel
    particularly
    pastime
    perceive
    perform
    permanent

13. permissible
    perseverance
    persistent
    personally
    playwright
    possession
    preceding
    prejudice
    prevalent
    primitive

14. privilege
    procedure
    proceed
    professor
    psychology
    pursue
    questionnaire
    receive
    recommend
    religious

15. reminisce
    repetition
    restaurant
    rhythm
    ridiculous
    sacrifice
    sacrilegious
    schedule
    secretary
    seize

16. sense
    sensible
    separate
    sergeant
    shining
    similar
    sincerely
    sophomore
    souvenir
    strength

17. superintendent
    supposed to
    suppression
    surprise
    synonym
    temperature
    tendency
    tragedy
    truly
    twelfth

18. tyranny
    unnecessary
    unusually
    used to*
    vacuum
    vengeance
    villain
    weird
    writing
    written

*See also U, pages 74–92.

USAGE

Certain words are frequently misused, often being confused with others that they resemble. Other words and expressions are generally considered unsuitable for formal writing and speaking; these include **colloquialisms** (expressions suitable for informal use only), **regionalisms** (those known only in certain areas), and **slang** (those used only among certain social groups and usually short-lived). Still other expressions are considered **nonstandard** or **illiterate** (always to be avoided). Authorities may disagree on the extent to which some words are acceptable. Consider any leading dictionary a reliable guide.

U.   Use the Right Word

a, an.   Use *a* before a word beginning with a consonant sound: *a c*ar, *a h*at, *a h*istory test, *a u*nion (*u* pronounced as if preceded by consonant *y*).
Use *an* before a word beginning with a vowel sound: *an a*ccident, *an i*mage, *an* honest person (*h* is silent), *an u*ncle.

accept, except.   *Accept* (verb) means "to receive": She *accepted* the gift.
Except (usually preposition) means "excluding": Everyone clapped *except* Farley.
NOTE: Except is occasionally a verb, meaning "to exclude": If you *except* the fifth clause, the rule applies in her case.

actual fact.   See *fact.*

adapt, adopt.   *Adapt* means "to adjust or make suitable." It is usually followed by *to:* He *adapted to* his new social environment.
Adopt means "to take as one's own": He *adopted* the habits of his new social environment. They *adopted* a child.

advice, advise.   *Advice* (noun) means "counsel": Take my *advice.*
Advise (verb) means "to give advice": I *advise* you to go.

affect, effect.   Most commonly, *affect* (verb) means "to influence": The war *affected* everyone.
Most commonly, *effect* (noun) means "a result": One *effect* of the war was mass starvation.
NOTE: Less commonly, *affect* (as a verb) means "to pretend or imitate": He *affected* a British accent. *Effect* (as a verb) means "to accomplish, to bring about": The medicine *effected* a cure.

aggravate.   Colloquial when used for *irritate* or *annoy:* The children *annoyed* (not *aggravated*) him.

aisle, isle. An *aisle* is a passage between rows of seats. An *isle* is an island.

all, all of. *All of* is redundant when used with common nouns: *All* (not *all of*) the men arrived on time.

allusion, illusion, delusion. *Allusion* means "an indirect reference": Her Biblical *allusions* drew praise.

Illusion means "a false perception eventually recognized as false": It was an optical *illusion.*

Delusion refers to a false perception or belief that is held as a result of self-deception: He labored under the *delusion* that everyone admired him.

almost. See *most.*

a lot, alot, allot. *A lot* is colloquial when used for *many* or *much:* He had *many* (not *a lot of*) relatives. He was *much* (not *a lot*) better. Avoid the misspelling *alot.*

Allot means "to apportion or give by some plan": The officials will *allot* each large family a subsidy.

already, all ready. Use *all ready* (meaning "completely ready") wherever *ready* alone makes sense: The squad was *all ready.* (The squad was *ready.*)

Elsewhere, use *already* (meaning "previously" or "by this time"): She had *already* eaten. He is here *already.*

alright. Incorrect for *all right.*

altogether, all together. Use *all together* (meaning "in a group") wherever *together* alone makes sense: We were *all together* at the party. (We were *together* at the party.)

Elsewhere, use *altogether* (meaning "wholly, completely, in all"): Custer was *altogether* surprised at Little Big Horn.

alumna, alumnus. An *alumna* is a female former student of a school or college. The plural is *alumnae* (usually pronounced with a final sound of *EE*).

An *alumnus* is the male or mixed-gender equivalent; the plural is *alumni* (usually pronounced with a final sound of *EYE*).

always. Do not contradict *always* (meaning "all the time") by adding *generally* or *usually* (meaning "most of the time") as a modifier.

Wrong: She *generally* (or *usually*) *always* wins.
Right: She *always* (or *usually* or *generally*) wins.

among. See *between.*

amoral, immoral. *Amoral* means "not concerned with morality": An infant's acts are *amoral.*

Immoral means "against morality": Murder is *immoral.*

amount, number. *Amount* refers to things in bulk or mass: a large *amount* of grain; no *amount* of persuasion.

Number refers to countable objects: a *number* of apples.

and etc. See *etc.*

and/or. Avoid it except in legal and business writing:

> Weak: Linda plans to get a degree in psychology *and/or* education.
> Better: Linda plans to get a degree in psychology, education, or both.

angry at, about, with. One becomes *angry at* or *about* a thing but *angry with* a person. See also *mad.*

ante-, anti-. Both are prefixes. *Ante-* means "before": *anteroom, antedate. Anti-* means "against": *antibody, antisocial.*

anxious, eager. *Anxious* conveys worry or unease: She is *anxious* about her safety.

> *Eager* conveys strong desire: He is *eager* to eat.

anymore, any more. *Any more* means "additional": Are there *any more* noodles?

> *Anymore* means "at present": You don't call *anymore.*

anyone, any one. *Anyone* means "any person": Has *anyone* here seen Kelly?

> *Any one* refers to any single item of a number of items: If you like my drawings, take *any one* you wish.

anyone, everyone, someone, anybody, everybody, somebody. Use a singular verb and pronoun with these words. See G-9.1E, page 29, and G-9.2B, page 31.

anyplace, everyplace, noplace, someplace. Colloquial. Precise writers and speakers prefer *anywhere, everywhere, nowhere, somewhere.*

anyways. Nonstandard; use *anyway* or *any way.*

anywheres, everywheres, nowheres, somewheres. Nonstandard; use *anywhere, everywhere,* etc.

apt, likely, liable. *Apt* is used when probability is based on normal, habitual, or customary tendency: She is *apt* to blush when embarrassed.

> *Likely* indicates mere probability: It is *likely* to rain tomorrow.
> *Liable* indicates an undesirable or undesired risk: He's *liable* to harm himself by playing with a loaded gun.

aren't I. Obviously ungrammatical (*are I not*), though some authorities accept it in informal use. *Am I not* is the alternative.

as, because, since. To express cause, make *because* your first choice; it is most precise.

> *As* and *since* may be ambiguous, conveying either a time or cause relation: *Since* you left, I've been sick. *Since* is acceptable informally when there is no ambiguity. *As* is the least acceptable.

as, like. See *like.*

at. Redundant with *where: Where* is she? (not *Where* is she *at?*)

aural. See *verbal.*

awful, awfully. *Awful* is colloquial when used to mean "very bad, ugly, shocking": His language was *shocking* (not *awful*).

> *Awful* is incorrect when used adverbially to mean "very": That pizza was *very* (not *awful*) good.
> *Awfully* is colloquial when used to mean "very": Jan is *very* (not *awfully*) happy.

awhile. Do not use the adverb *awhile* after *for*. One may stay *awhile* (adverb), stay *a while* (noun), stay for *a while* (noun), but not for *awhile* (adverb).

bad, badly. *Badly* (adverb) is colloquial when used for *very much* or *greatly* or after a linking verb (*be, seem,* etc.; see G-5.1A–C, page 16): She wanted *very much* (not *badly*) to be there.

Bad (adjective) correctly follows a linking verb: I feel *bad*.

because. See *reason is because* and *as, because, since*.

being as (how), being that. Colloquial or nonstandard for *as, because,* or *since* (which see).

beside, besides. *Beside* (preposition) means "by the side of": A man was sitting *beside* me [in the seat next to mine].

Besides (preposition) means "in addition to" or "except": Only one man was sitting *besides* me [everyone else was standing]. As a conjunctive adverb, it means "in addition": He is ugly; *besides,* he is boorish.

better, had better. Always add *had* or its contraction, *'d,* before *better* when you mean *should* or *ought to:*

Wrong: You *better* milk the cows.
Right: You *had* (or You *'d*) better milk the cows.

between. A preposition; the objective case must follow it: *between* you and *me,* not *between* you and *I*.

between, among. *Between* implies *two* persons or things in a relationship; *among* implies *three or more:* Must I decide *between* cake and ice cream? The estate was divided *among* the five children.

born, borne. For all meanings of *bear* except "give birth," the past participle is *borne. Borne* is correct in this sense also when it follows *have* or precedes *by:* Mrs. Jackson had already *borne* six children. The half-sisters were *borne* by different mothers.

Born is the correct past participle in other contexts relating to birth: The child was *born* in Brazil.

brake, break. *Brake* refers to stopping: Apply the *brake. Brake* the car carefully.

Break refers to destroying, damaging, exceeding, or interrupting: Don't *break* the glass. I'll *break* the record. Take a ten-minute *break*.

bring, take. Precise usage requires *bring* when you mean "to come (here) with" and *take* when you mean "to go (there) with."

bunch. Colloquial when meaning "crowd; group of people." Say "a *bunch* of bananas" but not "a *bunch* of friends."

bust, busted, bursted. Incorrect forms of the verb *burst,* of which the three principal parts are *burst, burst, burst:* Yesterday the water pipes *burst* (or *had burst*).

but that, but what. Colloquial for *that:* I don't doubt *that* (not *but that*) he'll come.

but yet. Redundant; use either alone: old *but* good; old *yet* good.

can, may. *Can* means "to be able": *Can* he lift the log? *May* means "to have permission": *May* I go with you?

can't hardly, can't scarcely. A double negative. Say "I *can't* hear her" or "I *can hardly* (or *can scarcely*) hear her."

can't help but. Colloquial for *can't help:*

Colloquial: I *can't help but* admire him.
Formal: I *can't help* admiring him.

canvas, canvass. A *canvas* is a cloth: Buy a *canvas* tent.
Canvass means "to solicit": *Canvass* the area for votes.

capital, capitol. Use *capitol* for the building where a legislature meets: The senator posed on the steps of the state *capitol.*
Elsewhere, use *capital:* Albany is the state *capital* [chief city]. The firm has little *capital* [money]. It was a *capital* [first-rate] idea. The defendant has committed a *capital* offense [one punishable by death].

carat, caret, carrot. Gold and gems are weighed in *carats.*
A *caret* (∧) signals an omission: I ∧ going home.
A *carrot* is a vegetable: Eat your *carrots.*

casual, causal. *Casual* means "occurring by chance, informal, un-planned"; *causal* means "involving cause."

censor, censure. To *censor* is to examine written, filmed, or broadcast material to delete objectionable content: How dare you *censor* my article!
To *censure* is to criticize or blame: The officer was *censured* for misconduct.

cite, site, sight. *Cite* means "quote an authority or give an example": He will *cite* Shakespeare's sonnet about age.
Site means "location": Here is the new building *site.*
Sight refers to seeing: His *sight* was failing. They have *sighted* the enemy.

classic, classical. *Classic* means "of the highest class or quality": *War and Peace* is a *classic* novel.
Classical means "pertaining to the art and life of ancient Greece and Rome": Mae is in Greece studying *classical* art. *Classical* music refers to symphonies, opera, and the like.

coarse, course. *Coarse* means "rough, not fine": *coarse* wool.
A *course* is a path or a series of lessons: race *course,* art *course.*

compare to, compare with. *Compare to* means "to point out one or more similarities": Sports writers are *comparing* the rookie *to* Hank Aaron.
Compare with means "to examine in order to find similarities and differences": Have you *compared* the new Ford *with* the Plymouth?

compliment, complement. *Compliment* means "to express praise": He *complimented* Beatrice on her good taste.
Complement means "to complete, enhance, or bring to perfection": The illustrations should *complement* the text.
The nouns *compliment* and *complement* are distinguished similarly.

comprise, compose, include. *Comprise* means "to be made up of (in entirety)": New York City *comprises* five boroughs.

Compose means the opposite, "to make up": Five boroughs *compose* New York City.

Include means "to contain (but not necessarily in entirety)": New York City *includes* the boroughs of Brooklyn and Queens.

connect up. See *up.*

consensus. Avoid the trite and redundant *consensus of opinion.* Use *consensus* alone ("general agreement").

contact. *Contact* as a verb meaning "to get in touch with" is still not acceptable in formal writing. *Contact* as a noun meaning "source" has become accepted.

continual, continuous. *Continual* means "frequently repeated": He worked in spite of *continual* interruptions.

Continuous means "without interruption": We heard the *continuous* roar of the falls.

continued on. Often redundant; omit *on:* We *continued* (not *continued on*) our journey. But: We *continued on* Highway 280.

convince, persuade. *Convince* emphasizes changing a person's belief: *Convince* me of your sincerity.

Persuade emphasizes moving a person to action: The officer's speech *persuaded* Pat to enlist.

correspond to, correspond with. *Correspond to* means "to be similar or analogous to": Our Congress *corresponds to* the British Parliament.

Correspond with means "to be in agreement or conformity with": Her actions did not *correspond with* her intentions.

Correspond with also means "to communicate with through exchange of letters."

could of, might of, ought to of, should of, would of. All wrong; *of* results from mishearing the contraction *'ve* (*have*). Write *could have, would have,* etc.

council, counsel, consul. *Council* means "a deliberative assembly of persons": The city *council* convenes at noon.

Counsel (noun) means "advice" or "attorney": He gave me good *counsel* when he told me to stop procrastinating. The *counsel* for the defense filed an appeal.

Counsel (verb) means "to give advice": He will *counsel* me about postgraduate plans.

Consul means "an officer in the foreign service": The distinguished guest was the *consul* from Spain.

credible, credulous, creditable. *Credible* means "believable": A good witness should be *credible.*

Credulous means "too ready to believe; gullible": A *credulous* person is easily duped.

Creditable means "praiseworthy": The young pianist gave a *creditable* performance of a difficult work.

data, phenomena, strata, media. These are plural forms: Those *data* are available. The singular forms are *datum* (rarely used), *phenomenon, stratum, medium.*
NOTE: Data is gaining acceptance also as singular when it refers to a single mass of information: All your *data* has been lost.

decent, descent. *Decent* means "proper, right": It's the *decent* thing to do.
Descent means "a going down" or "ancestry": The *descent* was steep. She's of Welsh *descent.*

delusion. See *allusion.*

device, devise. A *device* (noun) is an invention or a piece of equipment: I made this *device.*
To *devise* (verb) is to invent: *Devise* a new mousetrap.

different from, different than. Formal usage requires *different from:* Her dress is *different from* yours. The tendency is growing, however, to accept *different than* when a clause follows, since it seems simpler: His response was *different than* (rather than *different from what*) I expected.

differ from, differ with. *Differ from* expresses unlikeness: This book *differs from* the others in giving more details.
Differ with expresses divergence of opinion: I *differ with* you about the importance of the tax bill.

discuss, discus, disgust. To *discuss* is to talk: Let's *discuss* the election.
A *discus* is a disc-shaped object: Throw the *discus.*
Disgust refers to being offensive: War *disgusts* me.

disinterested, uninterested. *Uninterested* means simply "not interested": Pat is *uninterested* in mechanics.
Disinterested means "not influenced by personal interest; impartial, unbiased": Only a truly *disinterested* person should serve as an arbitrator.

dived, dove. *Dived* is the preferred past tense and past participle of *dive:* The youngsters *dived* (not *dove*) for coins.

due (to). *Due to* is in common use as a preposition. However, strict usage requires *because of:* We were late *because of* (not *due to*) traffic.
Due is correct as an adjective following a linking verb: Our lateness was *due* to traffic.
See also *fact that.*

each and every. Redundant; use either: *"each* of us," *"every* one of us," but not *"each and every* one of us."

each other, one another. *Each other* refers to *two* persons or things, *one another* to *three or more.*

eager. See *anxious.*

effect. See *affect.*

elicit, illicit. To *elicit* is to draw forth; *Elicit* some response.
Illicit means "illegal": Shun *illicit* drugs.

emigrate, immigrate. *Emigrate* means "to leave a country"; *immigrate* means "to enter a new country": Millions *emigrated* from Europe. They *immigrated* to America.

eminent, imminent. *Eminent* means "distinguished": She's an *eminent* surgeon.
 Imminent means "about to happen": Rain is *imminent*.

end up. See *up*.

ensure, insure. Use *insure* when referring to insurance (protection against loss): You should *insure* your house.
 Ensure is often preferred for "make sure, make safe": These tires will *ensure* that you'll never skid.

enthuse. Colloquial for *become enthusiastic:* She *becomes enthusiastic* (not *enthuses*) about everything.

envelop, envelope. To *envelop* is to surround: Fog *envelops* us.
 An *envelope* holds a letter: Seal the *envelope*.

etc. Avoid *etc.* (meaning "and others") in formal paragraph writing. Use *and others* or *and so forth*. Better, rephrase the sentence to avoid all of these:
 Weak: Jill prefers reading Twain, Howells, *and so forth*.
 Better: Jill prefers writers *such as* Twain and Howells.

 Always avoid *and etc.;* it is redundant.

everybody. See *anyone*.

everyone, every one. Use *everyone* where you can substitute *everybody: Everyone* (*everybody*) wishes you well. Elsewhere, use *every one* (usually followed by *of*): *Every one* of the roses died. See also *anyone*.

everyplace, everywheres. See *anyplace, anywheres*.

every so often. Colloquial for *occasionally*. Also colloquial: *every which way, every bit as, every once in a while*.

except. See *accept*.

fact. *Actual fact, real fact,* and *true fact* are usually redundant.

fact that. Wordy. For *due to the fact that,* say *because;* for *except for the fact that,* say *except that;* or recast the sentence:
 Wordy: *Due to the fact that he was late,* we lost.
 Concise: We lost *because he was late*.
 Wordy: *The fact that he was late* made us lose.
 Concise: *His lateness* made us lose.

famous, notable, notorious. *Famous* means "widely known"; it usually has favorable connotations.
 Notable means "worthy of note" or "prominent"; a person can be *notable* without being *famous*.
 Notorious means "widely known in an unfavorable way": Bluebeard was *notorious* for being a bad husband.

farther, further. *Farther* refers to distance: He walked *farther* than I did.
 Further means "to a greater extent or degree": Let's discuss the matter *further*.

fewer, less. Use *fewer* with countable things; *fewer* refers to number: She has *fewer* assets than I have.

Use *less* with things that are not countable but are considered in bulk or mass; *less* refers to quantity: She has *less* wealth than I have.

fine. The adjective *fine* is much overused as a vague word of approval, as "a *fine* boy." Use a more precise word. As an adverb meaning "well" ("He does *fine*"), it is colloquial. *Fine* also means "subtle" or "not coarse."

folks. Colloquial for *family, relatives, people.*

formally, formerly. *Formally* means "according to proper form": Introduce us *formally*.

Formerly means "previously": They *formerly* lived here.

former, first; latter, last. *Former* and *latter* refer to the first and second named of two; *first* and *last* refer to items in a series.

forth, fourth. *Forth* means "forward": Go *forth* and conquer.

Fourth is 4th: I was *fourth* in line.

funny. Do not use in formal writing to mean "odd" or "peculiar."

generally always. See *always.*

good. Do not use this adjective for the adverb *well:* The car runs *well* (not *good*).

As an adjective, *good* may correctly follow a linking verb: She feels *good* about winning. See G-5.1A–C, page16–17.

got. See *have got.*

had of. Incorrect for *had:* I wish I *had* (or *I'd*—not *I had of* or *I'd of*) seen the show.

had ought. Incorrect for *ought:* I *ought* (not *had ought*) to go.

Hadn't ought is also incorrect. Use *ought not.*

half. Say *a half* or *half a(n),* not *a half a(n):* Fill *a half* page (or *half a* page, but not *a half a* page).

hanged, hung. *Hanged* means "executed": Judas *hanged* himself.

Hung means "suspended": The picture was *hung.*

hardly. See *can't hardly.*

have got. Colloquial for *have:* I *have* (not *have got*) a dollar.

healthy, healthful. *Healthy* means "possessing health": The children are *healthy.*

Healthful means "conducive to health": Good food is *healthful.*

help. See *can't help but.*

herself, himself, myself, yourself. Do not substitute these intensive pronouns for the personal pronouns *I, you, him, her:* Grace and *you* (not *yourself*) are invited. She sent tickets to Don and *me* (not *myself*). See G-6.1E, page 20.

hisself. Incorrect for *himself:* He blames *himself* (not *hisself*) for the accident. See G-6.1E, page 20.

historic, historical. Strictly, *historic* means "famous or important in history": July 4, 1776, is a *historic* date.
Historical means "pertaining to history": Verna reads *historical* novels.

hopefully. Strictly, it means "full of hope": Christy *hopefully* awaited the posting of grades. In formal use, avoid it in the sense of "it is hoped that": *We hope that* (not *Hopefully*) the train will arrive on time.

how. See *being as* (*how*), *seeing as how*.

if, whether. *If* can be unclear when used to introduce alternative conditions. "Tell us *if* you see him" can mean not only "Tell us *whether* (*or not*) you see him" but also "*In case* you ever see him, tell us." Use *whether* for clarity.

illicit. See *elicit*.

illusion. See *allusion*.

immigrate. See *emigrate*.

imminent. See *eminent*.

immoral. See *amoral*.

imply, infer. The writer or speaker *implies;* the reader or listener *infers.*
Imply means "to state indirectly or suggest": He *implied* that we were at fault.
Infer means "to draw a conclusion or derive by reasoning": I *inferred* from his statement that he blamed us.

in, into. *Into* indicates movement from outside to inside: Fido ran *into* the house.
Otherwise, use *in:* Fido stays *in* the house at night.

in back of. Colloquial for *behind, at the back of, back of.*

include. See *comprise*.

incredible, incredulous. A fact or happening is *incredible* (unbelievable): Her thirty-foot putt was *incredible.*
A person is *incredulous* (unbelieving): He was *incredulous* when told of her thirty-foot putt.

individual, person, party. Do not use *party* or *individual* when you mean simply *person: A person* (not *an individual* or *a party)* that I met told me the news.
Except in legal and telephone-company language, and when you mean "one taking part," do not use *party* to refer to one person.
Use *individual* only when emphasizing a person's singleness: Will you act with the group or as an *individual?*

ingenious, ingenuous. *Ingenious* means "clever"; *ingenuous* means "naive, frank."

in regards to. Incorrect for *in regard to, with regard to,* or *as regards.*

inside of. Often redundant; omit *of* or use *within:* He was *inside* (not *inside of*) the room.

Inside of is colloquial when used in reference to time or distance: I shall come *within* (not *inside of*) an hour. I was *within* (not *inside of*) a mile of my destination.

"The *inside* of the house" is correct; here *inside* is a noun.

instance, instant, instant's. *Instance* means "a case or example": He cited an *instance* of discrimination.

Instant (noun) means "a brief time, a particular point in time, a moment": Come here this *instant!*

Instant (adjective) means "urgent or immediate": An *instant* need is food for the poor. Do you like *instant* coffee?

Instant's is the possessive form of the noun *instant:* He came at an *instant's* notice.

insure. See *ensure.*

irregardless. There is no such word. Use *regardless.*

irrelevant. This word means "not related to the point or subject." Notice the letters *rel* as in *related.* There is no such word as *irrevelant.*

isle. See *aisle.*

is when, is where. Avoid both expressions except when referring to a time or place:

> Wrong: A treaty *is when* nations sign an agreement.
> Right: A treaty *is* a signed agreement among nations.
> Right: Home *is where* the heart is. [place]

it being. An awkward substitute for *since it is.*

its, it's. *Its* is the possessive of *it:* The dog wagged *its* tail.

It's is the contraction of *it is.* Use *it's* only if you can correctly substitute *it is* in your sentence: *It's* (*It is*) the best thing.

kid, kids. Colloquial for *child, children.*

kind of, sort of. Colloquial if used for *somewhat* or *rather.*

kind of a, sort of a. Omit the *a.* He wanted *some kind of* (not *some kind of a*) book.

last, latter. See *former.*

later, latter. *Later,* the comparative form of *late,* means "more late."

Latter refers to the second of two things mentioned. If more than two are mentioned, use *last* instead of *latter.*

lay. See *lie.*

lead, led. *Lead* (rhymes with *need*) is the present tense of the verb meaning "to conduct, to go at the head of, to show the way": She can *lead* us to safety.

Led is the past tense and past participle of the same verb: She *led* us to safety. She has *led* us to safety.

Lead (rhymes with *dead*) is a metal: I need a *lead* pipe.

learn, teach. *Learn* means "to acquire knowledge": We *learned* irregular verbs.

Teach means "to impart knowledge": The professor *taught* us irregular verbs.

leave, let. *Leave* means "to depart": I must *leave* now.
Let means "to permit": *Let* me go.

less. See *fewer.*

lessen, lesson. To *lessen* is to diminish: His pain *lessened.*
A *lesson* is a unit of learning: Study your *lesson.*

liable, likely. See *apt.*

lie, lay. Lie means "to rest" and is an intransitive verb (it never takes an object): He makes me *lie* down in green pastures. The islands *lie* under the tropical sun. Here *lies* Jeremiah Todd.

Lay means "to put, to place," and is a transitive verb (it must take an object): *Lay* your *head* on this pillow. Let me *lay* your *fears* to rest.

To complicate matters, the past tense of *lie* is spelled and pronounced the same as the present tense of *lay:*

Present	Past	Past Participle
lie [rest]	lay [rested]	(has) lain [rested]
lay [place]	laid [placed]	(has) laid [placed]

Yesterday Sandra *lay* [*rested*] too long in the sun. She should not have *lain* [*rested*] there so long.

Yesterday the workers *laid* [*placed*] the foundation. They have *laid* [*placed*] it well.

like, as. In formal English, do not use *like* (preposition) where *as* or *as if* (conjunction) sounds right: He looks *as if* (not *like*) he's angry. She died just *as* (not *like*) her mother did.

loose, lose. *Loose* (usually adjective—rhymes with *goose*) is the opposite of *tight* or *confined:* A *loose* coupling caused the wreck. The lions are *loose!*

Loose is also sometimes a verb: *Loose* my bonds.

Lose (verb—rhymes with *news*) is the opposite of *to find* or *win:* Did you *lose* your wallet? We may *lose* the game.

lots, lots of. Colloquial if used for *much* or *many.*

mad, angry. In formal English, do not use *mad* to mean "angry." The common formal meaning of *mad* is "insane" or "insanely foolish": Do not be *angry* with me (not *mad* at me).

marvelous. Overused as a vague word of approval.

may. See *can.*

maybe, may be. *Maybe* is an adverb meaning "perhaps": *Maybe* you should ask her. Do not confuse it with the verb *may be:* He *may be* arriving late tonight.

media. See *data.*

meet up with. See *up.*

might of. See *could of.*

moral, morale. *Moral* (as an adjective) means "righteous, ethical": To pay his debts was a *moral* obligation.

Moral (as a noun) means "a lesson or truth taught in a story": The *moral* of the story is that greed is wrong.

Morale is a noun meaning "spirit": The team's *morale* sagged.

most, almost. Do not use the adjective *most* for the adverb *almost. Almost* (not *most*) all my friends came.

myself. See *herself.*

nauseated, nauseous. *Nauseated* means "suffering from nausea": I was *nauseated* from the fumes.

Nauseous means "causing nausea": The *nauseous* fumes overcame me.

nice. Trite and overused as a substitute for *pleasant* or *agreeable* or for indicating approval. Use a specific adjective.

noplace, nowheres. See *anyplace; anywheres.*

notable, notorious. See *famous.*

nowhere near. Colloquial for *not nearly.*

number. See *amount.*

of. See *could of; kind of; kind of a; off of; outside of.*

off of. Usually redundant; omit *of:* Keep *off* (not *off of*) the grass. He jumped *off* (not *off of*) the platform.

O.K., okay. Colloquial for *all right* or *correct.*

one another. See *each other.*

only. Place *only* as close as possible to the word it modifies, to prevent misreading. "I *only lent* her those books" and "I lent her *only those* books" have different meanings.

or. See *and/or.*

oral. See *verbal.*

ought to of. See *could of; had ought.*

outside of. Colloquial for *besides, except. Of* is redundant when denoting space: She was *outside* (not *outside of*) the store. But "the *outside of* the house" is correct; here *outside* is a noun.

over with. Redundant; omit *with.*

party, person. See *individual.*

passed, past. *Passed* (verb) is from *pass:* I *passed* the test.

Past (noun) means "a former time": Forget the *past.*

Past (preposition) means "by, beyond": Walk *past* the gate.

percent (per cent), percentage. Use *percent* (or *per cent*) with a specific figure: 45 *percent.* Otherwise, use *percentage:* a small *percentage* of voters.

personal, personnel. *Personal* means "private": It was a *personal* question.

Personnel are employees: Notify all *personnel.*

persuade. See *convince*.

phenomena. See *data*.

plan on. Do not use in formal English for *plan to:* I *plan to go* (not *plan on going*).

plenty. Colloquial when used as an adverb: His excuse was *quite* (not *plenty*) good enough for me.
Plenty is correct as a noun: We have *plenty* of food.

plus. In general writing, avoid using *plus* for *and:* Jill *and* (not *plus*) all her friends saw you. Jill saw you, *and* (not *plus*) she heard you sing.

practical, practicable. *Practical* means "useful, sensible, not theoretical"; *practicable* means "feasible, capable of being put into practice": Because they were *practical* women, they submitted a plan that was *practicable*.

precede, proceed. To *precede* is to come before: *X precedes Y*.
Proceed means "to go forward": The parade *proceeded*.

presence, presents. *Presence* means "being present; attendance": Demand their *presence*.
Presents are gifts, such as birthday *presents*.

pretty. Colloquial for *large:* The accident will cost him a *large* (not *pretty*) sum.

principle, principal. A *principle* is a rule or a truth (remember: *principLE* = *ruLE*): The Ten Commandments are moral *principles*. The Pythagorean theorem is a mathematical *principle*.
Elsewhere, use *principal,* meaning "chief, chief part, chief person": All *principal* roads are closed. At 8 percent, your *principal* will earn $160 interest. The *principal* praised the students.

provided, providing. Use *provided* (*that*) in preference to *providing* (*that*) when you mean "on the specific condition that": She will donate twenty dollars *provided that* (not *providing that*) her employer matches it.

quiet, quite. *Quiet* means "not noisy": This motor is *quiet*.
Quite means "very, completely": I'm not *quite* ready.

raise, rise. *Raise, raised, raised* ("to lift, make come up") is a transitive verb (takes an object): He *raises vegetables*. He *raised* the *window*.
Rise, rose, risen ("to ascend") is an intransitive verb (never has an object): The sun is *rising*.

range, vary. *Range* means "to change or differ within limits": Applicants *ranged* in age from nineteen to thirty years.
Vary means "to change or differ": Applicants *varied* in age.

real. Colloquial when used for the adverb *really* or *very:* She was *very* (not *real*) brave.

reason is because. Redundant. Use *that* instead: The reason he is late is *that* (not *because*) he overslept. Or say *He is late because he overslept*.

regardless, regards. See *irregardless; in regards to*.

respectfully, respectively. *Respectfully* means "in a manner showing respect": He bowed *respectfully* before the queen. *Respectfully* yours.

Respectively means "each in the order given": First and second prizes were awarded to Luann and Juan, *respectively.*

Reverend. Never use *Reverend* alone as a form of address. The title *Reverend* is properly preceded by *the* and is followed by *Mr., Ms., Dr.,* or the first name or initials of the person referred to: We met *the Reverend* Charles Harris (or *the Reverend Mr. Harris*).

right. Colloquial or archaic when used to mean "directly" or "very": She went *directly* (not *right*) home. He was *very* (not *right*) tired.

right, rite, write. *Right* means "correct": the *right* answer.
A *rite* is a ceremony, such as an initiation *rite.*
To *write* is to put words on paper: *Write* us from Hawaii.

same. Unless writing a legal document, avoid using *same* for *it* or *them:* We visited Maine and found *it* (not *same*) delightful.

scarcely. See *can't hardly.*

seeing as how, seeing that. Incorrect for *since* or *because.*

seldom ever. Redundant and incorrect for *seldom, hardly ever, seldom if ever, seldom or never.*

shape. Colloquial if used for *condition:* He was in poor *condition* (not *shape*).

should of. See *could of.*

sight, site. See *cite.*

since. See *as, because, since.*

sit, set. *Sit, sat, sat* is an intransitive verb (has no object); it means "to be seated": I *sat* on the floor.
Set, set, set is a transitive verb (has an object); it means "to put or place": She *set* the *dishes* on the table.
(*Set* has several intransitive senses, but it is equivalent to *sit* only when one speaks of a hen that *sets* on her eggs.)

so. *So* is informal when used to introduce a main clause; in formal writing, use *thus* or *therefore,* or recast the sentence:
Informal: All the crew died, *so* the ship was lost.
Formal: All the crew died; *thus* the ship was lost.
Recast: The ship was lost *because* all the crew died.
Avoid *so* for *very:* I am *very* (not *so*) happy.
Avoid using *so* for *so that* in clauses of purpose: She came *so that* (not *so*) she might help.

some. Colloquial if used for *somewhat, a little,* or *quite:* He worried *somewhat* (not *some*). He's *quite a* (not *some*) golfer!

somebody, someone. See *anyone.*

someplace, somewheres. See *anyplace; anywheres.*

sort of, sort of a. See *kind of; kind of a; these kind.*

stationary, stationery. *Stationary* means "not moving, not movable": This machine is *stationary.*
Stationery is writing paper.

strata. See *data*.

such, no such a. *Such* is colloquial when used for *very:* It is *such* a lovely day. Better: It is a *very* lovely day.

When *such* suggests "what kind" or "how much," it is followed in formal writing by a clause specifying the degree or kind: It was *such* a lovely day *that we went on a picnic*. There was *such* crowding *that we came home*.

No such a is incorrect for *no such*. There is *no such* (not *no such a*) place.

sure. Do not use the adjective *sure* for the adverb *surely* or *certainly:* I *surely* (not *sure*) admire her.

Colloquial: "Are you going?" *"Sure."*

sure and. See *try and*.

take. See *bring*.

take and, went and. Redundant: She *hit* (not *took and hit* or *went and hit*) the ball.

teach. See *learn*.

terribly. Colloquial when used for *extremely* or *very:* It's *very* (not *terribly*) late.

than, then. *Than* is a conjunction suggesting difference: He is taller *than* I (am tall). See also *different from*.

Then is an adverb meaning "at that time," "next," or "in that case": *Then* we shall go.

that. See *being that; but that; seeing that; this; this here; who*.

their, there, they're. *Their* is a possessive pronoun: It is *their* turn.

There is an adverb referring to place: Sit *there*. It is also an expletive (an introductory word): *There* are four of us.

They're is a contraction of *they are: They're* on their way.

them. Do not use for *those:* Watch *those* (not *them*) cars!

these kind, these sort. *Kind* and *sort* are singular nouns. Do not modify them with the plurals *these* and *those*. Use the singular *this* or *that* instead: I prefer *this* (not *these*) kind of fish. *That* (not *those*) sort of fish will make me sick.

thing. Avoid this vague noun where you can use a more specific one: Her next *point* (not *The next thing she said*) concerned economic benefits.

this, that, which. Use only to refer to a definite antecedent. See G-6.3B, page 23.

this here, that there, these here, those there. Nonstandard for *this, that, these, those*.

those kind, those sort. See *these kind*.

threw, through. *Threw* is the past of *throw*. I *threw* the ball.

Through means "from end to end of." See also next entry.

through, thorough, thought. *Through* means "from end to end or side to side of": *through* the tunnel.

Thorough means "complete, exact": a *thorough* search.
Thought refers to thinking: a clever *thought*.

thusly.   Incorrect for *thus*.

to, too, two.   *To* is a preposition: She came *to* class. *To* also introduces an infinitive: I wanted *to* hear him.

Too is an adverb meaning "also" or expressing degree: She laughed *too*. He was *too* sick to work. Do not use *too* for *very*: He wasn't *very* (not *too*) happy.

Two is a number: I have *two* books.

toward, towards.   Use either, but be consistent.

try and, sure and.   Incorrect for *try to* and *sure to: Try to* (not *Try and*) come. Be *sure to* (not *sure and*) call me.

-type.   Avoid needless or illogical use of *-type* as a suffix: She wanted a reflex (not *reflex-type*) camera.

uninterested.   See *disinterested*.

unique.   *Unique* means "having no like or equal." Do not use it with *more, most, very,* or the like: The design was *unique* (not *most unique*).

up.   Often redundant after a verb. Drop *up* unless dropping it changes your meaning: Connect (not *connect up*) the pipes. This road ends (not *ends up*) in a swamp. Climb (not *climb up*) that hill. Gerry met (not *met up with*) difficulties.

usage, utilize, use.   *Usage* and *utilize* sound overblown if used where the simple *use* (noun or verb) will do. *Usage* means only "customary use or practice": The book explains English *usage*. *Utilize* means only "to put to some practical or special use": *Utilize* my cane as a splint. Otherwise, stay with *use*.

used to.   The spelling is *used to*, except after *did:* They *used to* date. The flag *used to* have forty-eight stars. Didn't he *use to* smoke?

usually always.   See *always*.

vary.   See *range*.

verbal, oral, aural.   *Verbal* means "expressed in words, either written or spoken": An artist's expression may take pictorial, plastic, *verbal,* or other form. (For the grammatical term *verbal,* see G-4.3D, page13.)

Oral means "uttered or spoken": He gave an *oral* report.

Aural refers to hearing ("of or perceived by the ear").

very.   Do not use this adverb to modify a past participle directly. Use *very* + an adverb such as *much, well:* Her singing was *very much* appreciated (not *very* appreciated).

Avoid overuse of *very*. *Extremely* and *quite* are good synonyms: She was *quite* (not *very*) embarrassed.

wait on.   *Wait on* means "to attend or serve." It is colloquial if used to mean *wait for:* I waited *for* (not *on*) a bus.

way, ways.   *Way* is colloquial if used for *far:* He lives *far* (not *way*) across the valley.

Way is colloquial in reference to health: She is *in poor health* (not *in a bad way*).

Ways is colloquial for *way* when indicating distance: She lives a little *way* (not *ways*) down the road.

weak, week. *Weak* means "not strong": *weak* from the flu.
A *week* is seven days.

weather, whether. *Weather* refers to rain, sunshine, etc.
Whether introduces alternatives: *whether* we live or die.

weird. Slang when used for *strange, unusual.*

well. See *good.*

went and. See *take and.*

what. See *but what.*

where. Incorrect when used for *that.* I read in the paper *that* (not *where*) she had arrived.

where . . . at. See *at.*

whether. See *if; weather.*

which. See *this; who.*

while. The strict meaning of *while* is "during the time that." Avoid using it to mean *though* or *whereas: A* century ago many criminals were executed in America, *whereas* (not *while*) today very few are.

who, which, that. Use *who,* not *which,* when referring to people; *which* is only for things. *That* can refer to people or things: The people *who* (or *that,* but not *which*) live here are noisy.

Who may introduce either a restrictive or nonrestrictive clause (see P-1.1E(2), page 41, for definitions of these terms).

That introduces only restrictive clauses. Many authorities say that *which* should introduce only nonrestrictive clauses, as in "Healy Hall, *which* is on your right, was built in 1878."

who's, whose. *Who's* is a contraction of *who is: Who's* that?
Whose is the possessive of *who: Whose* hat is this?

with. See *over with.*

woman, women. *Woman,* like *man,* is singular: that *woman.*
Women, like *men,* is plural: those *women.*

wonderful. Trite and overused as an adjective of approval.

worst way. Incorrect for *very much:* I want *very much* to go (not *I want to go in the worst way*).

would have. Use *had,* not *would have,* in an *if* clause:

Wrong: If I *would have* known, I would have left earlier.
Right: If I *had* known, I would have left earlier.

would of. See *could of.*

write. See *right, rite, write.*

yet. See *but yet.*

you all. A southern regionalism for the plural *you.*

your, you're. *Your* is the possessive of *you:* Wear *your* hat. *You're* is a contraction of *you are: You're* late.

yourself. See *herself.*

you was. Nonstandard for *you were.*

BEYOND THE SENTENCE

Most sentences that you write will become parts of larger units of writing (paragraphs), and most paragraphs parts of still larger units (essays, letters, papers, articles, and the like). This section explains important matters of form in paragraphing, outlining, and documenting papers. For other matters of manuscript form, see M-1, page 58.

B-1. Paragraphing

A paragraph is a unit of written thought. Generally it contains several sentences clearly related in meaning, though sometimes for emphasis, or in dialog or transition, it may have only one or two sentences.

1. Parts of a Paragraph. A typical paragraph in the body of a paper has these elements:

A. The Topic Sentence. This sentence contains the main idea that the paragraph will develop. It most often comes first, though it may appear elsewhere—particularly at the end—or only be implied. Some longer paragraphs may restate the idea of an opening topic sentence in a closing summary sentence. In B-2 below, topic sentences are italicized.

B. Details. Details that support the main idea make up the body of a paragraph. These may be **facts, examples, reasons,** elements of a **definition** or an **explanation,** or points of **comparison** or **contrast** (see B-2 below—the unitalicized sentences are supporting details).

C. Words That Bind Paragraphs Together. Paragraphs **cohere** (hold together) best when the thought flows smoothly from the first sentence through the last, with relations between ideas clearly signaled or implied. Two devices that aid coherence are **transitional expressions** and **repetition** of key words or phrases.

(1) *Transitional expressions* indicate stages of thought (*first, second, consequently, finally*), signal further evidence (*in addition, moreover, next, also*), mark a change in direction (*however, yet, still, on the other hand, nevertheless*), show relationships (*above all, that is, in particular, then, meanwhile, at last, further*), or signal a conclusion (*therefore, thus, on the whole*). Avoid *firstly, secondly,* and the trite *in conclusion.* See B-2 below.

(2) *Repetition of key words.* Repeating certain words or phrases central to your topic gives your reader valuable signposts.

Repetitions may be in the identical words, in synonyms, or in pronouns. See B-2 below.

2. Sample Paragraphs.

Below are two sample body paragraphs. The topic sentence of each is *italicized;* transitional expressions and repeated key words or phrases are in **boldface**. The first paragraph is developed by comparisons and example; the second, by reasons supported with example.

Sometimes, of course, our [punctuation] markings may be simply a matter of aesthetics. Popping in a **comma** can be **like** slipping on the necklace that gives an outfit quiet elegance, **or like** catching the sound of running water that complements, as it completes, the silence of a Japanese landscape. **When** V.S. Naipaul, in his latest novel, writes, "He was a middle-aged man, with **glasses**," the first **comma** can seem a little precious. **Yet it** gives the description a spin, **as well as** a subtlety, that it otherwise lacks, **and it** shows that the **glasses** are **not** part of the middle-agedness, **but** something else.

—Pico Iyer,
"In Praise of the Humble Comma"

People who talk about **"correct English"** are usually oversimplifying the problem dangerously. There is no single, monolithic **"correct English."** There is nothing inherent or intrinsic that makes language **"correct."** **For instance**, in America it is considered low-class or "backwoodsy" to say "He **et** his dinner." In England, **however**, *et*, as the past tense of *eat*, has the highest prestige, **and** the best-spoken Englishmen will say "He **et** his dinner." It is simply a matter of **differing usage,** in one social group or another. Even good speakers have **several styles** at their command—**not only** the **formal English** of the purists, **but** an easy, **informal English** for conversational situations. *Good English is that which is appropriate and effective, **even when** it goes against the pronouncements of purists.*

—Allan Walker Reed,
"Is American English Deteriorating?"

3. Paragraphing Dialog and Other Quoted Material

In writing dialogue, start a new paragraph with each change of speaker (see example, P-8.1A(7), page 51). For uninterrupted quotations of more than one paragraph, see P-8.1A(3), page 51. For quotations within a paragraph, see M-1.4, page 59.

B-2.   Outlining

Multiparagraph papers usually call for some kind of written plan. It may be anything from a scratch jotting of topics to a formal outline. (Your instructor may require the latter.) Before you begin your outline or scratch plan, form a guiding sentence stating the purpose or the **thesis** of your paper. (A thesis is your central idea, or what you will show.) One way to form a thesis is to complete this sentence: *This paper will show that. . . .*

1. Types of Formal Outlines
A. Traditional (Roman Number)

(1) *Topic outline:* a listing of topics and subtopics arranged by relative importance and by intended order of appearance in the paper. Headings within the same division or subdivision must be in parallel structure (see G-10.1F, page 33); such structure helps you see clearly whether your topics are logically placed and related. Follow the numbering-lettering system in this sample:

Growing Up in a Large Family [Title]

Thesis: Though far from idyllic, an upbringing in a large family prepares one for a well-adjusted adulthood.

   I. Popular misconceptions of large-family life
      A. Fewer material benefits
      B. Less parental attention
  II. Benefits of a large-family upbringing
      B. Development of social maturity
         1. Learning from older siblings
         2. Teaching younger siblings
         3. Learning to get along with others
      C. Nondevelopment of undesirable traits
         1. Egocentrism
         2. Materialism
 III. Drawbacks of a large-family upbringing

      . . . and so forth.

(2) *Sentence outline:* a similar arrangement using complete sentences for each item:

I. Misconceptions about large-family life are widespread.
   A. Children may be deprived of material benefits.
   B. Parents can devote less attention to each child.

B. Decimal. A decimal outline (either topic or sentence) differs from a traditional outline only in its numbering system:

2. Benefits of a large-family upbringing
   2.1. Development of responsibility
      2.1.1. Household
      2.1.2. Financial
      2.1.3. Societal

2. Principles of Outlining
A. A Topic (or Sentence) Must Follow Every Letter or Number.

Wrong: I.
Right: I. Causes of the war

B. **It Is Illogical for a Topic (Heading) to Have a Single Subdivision.**

For every *A* there must be at least a *B;* for every *1* at least a *2*. If you can think of only one subdivision for a topic, do not divide it at all.

C. **An Outline Evolves with Its Paper.** Fill in items as they occur to you, and rearrange or drop them as needed until the final draft. Determine your primary headings before your secondary ones, your secondary before your tertiary.

B-3. Documentation

Research papers and scholarly articles for publication require **documentation** of all information and ideas you obtained from reference sources. Documentation consists of **citations** (acknowledgment, within your text, of sources of material you used) and a **reference list** (an alphabetical list, at the end of your paper, of sources of material you used—also called a *list of works cited* or a *bibliography*). Many papers in the humanities require the Modern Language Association (MLA) documentation style. Others, including those in history, require the Chicago Manual of Style (Chicago) format. Those in many social and physical sciences, education, business, and technology use the American Psychological Association (APA) style. Some instructors or publishers may require that you use still another style, that of the University of Chicago.

1. **Citations.**   You must state the sources of facts and ideas that you obtained from your research. You must tell enough about each source so that your reader can locate the information or idea you mention.

A. **The MLA Style.** If you cite a general idea of an entire work, just mention the author's name in your text (the body of your paper):

Robert Hughes shows how a highly civilized nation treated its convicts with appalling inhumanity.

If you quote or paraphrase a specific fact or idea from a source, cite in your text the author's name and the page from which the material came:

Robert Hughes observes that a half-century ago convict ancestry was "a stain to be hidden" (158). [direct quotation]

or

One recent historian of Australia's founding observes, "Fifty years ago, convict ancestry was a stain to be hidden" (Hughes 158). [direct quotation—omit author's first name in the parentheses] *or*

Robert Hughes observes that fifty years ago Australians were ashamed of convict ancestry (158). [paraphrase]

Your reader can find full information about the source by turning to your reference list:

Hughes, Robert. <u>The Fatal Shore</u>. New York: Knopf, 1986.

NOTE: If your reference list contains more than one entry by the same author(s), give the title (shortened) before the page number in your citation:

(Hughes, <u>Fatal Shore</u> 158).

B. The APA Style. If you cite a general idea of an entire work, mention the author(s) and year of publication in your text:

Gordon and Braun (1983) examined the effects of teaching story grammar.

or

A major study examined the effects of teaching story grammar (Gordon & Braun, 1983).

If you quote or paraphrase a specific fact or idea from a source, cite in your text the author's last name, the year of publication, and the page from which the material came:

Gordon and Braun (1983) define story grammars as "sets of rules that spell out how stories are typically organized" (p. 116).

or

One study defines story grammars as "sets of rules that spell out how stories are typically organized" (Gordon & Braun, 1983, p. 116).

Your reader can find full information about the source by turning to your reference list.

NOTE: If your reference list contains more than one entry by the same author(s) with the same publication date, list these entries alphabetically by title in your reference list, and in your citations assign each entry a letter in its reference-list order:

(Gordon & Braun, 1983a).

C. The Chicago Style. If you cite a general idea of an entire work, give publication information in a footnote (at the bottom of the page) or endnote (on a separate page entitled "Notes" at the end of the paper). Use a superscript (raised) number immediately after the sentence in which you refer to the idea. In the footnote, use the same superscript number before the publication information. In the end notes, the number preceding each entry can either be raised or set on the same line as the entry.

In the text:

Robert Hughes shows how a highly civilized nation treated its convicts with appalling inhumanity.[1]

In the footnote or endnote:

[1]Robert Hughes, The Fatal Shore (New York: Alfred A. Knopf, 1986).

Alternate style for endnote:

1. Robert Hughes, The Fatal Shore (New York: Alfred A. Knopf, 1986).

NOTE: In the footnote or endnote, the first line is indented five spaces.

If you quote or paraphrase a specific idea or fact from a source, the footnote or endnote also includes the page from which the material came:

In the text:

One recent historian of Australia's founding observes, "Fifty years ago, convict ancestry was a stain to be hidden."[1] [direct quotation]

or

Robert Hughes observes that fifty years ago Australians were ashamed of convict ancestry.[1] [paraphrase]

In the footnote or endnote:

[1]Robert Hughes, The Fatal Shore, (New York: Alfred A. Knopf, 1986), 158.

NOTE: If your notes contain more than one reference to a single work, the second and subsequent references need to include only the author's last name and the page number:

First note on Hughes:

[1]Robert Hughes, The Fatal Shore, (New York: Alfred A. Knopf, 1986), 158.

Second note on Hughes:

[5]Hughes, 209.

When two references to the same work are consecutive, *ibid.* ("in the same place") may take the place of the author's name and the title in the second reference:

First note on Hughes:

[1]Robert Hughes, The Fatal Shore, (New York: Alfred A. Knopf, 1986), 158.

Second note on Hughes:

[2]Ibid., 186.

Notes are arranged in numerical order. Both footnotes and endnotes are single-spaced within each entry and double-spaced between entries.

2. Reference List.

Normally, every source cited in your text must also be given in your reference list, and vice versa. Use the following forms for entries in a reference list. Alphabetize according to the last name of the author (or first author, if there are two or more). Indent the second and any additional lines of each entry five spaces in MLA and Chicago styles, three in APA (space limitations prevent showing full indentations in the following lists). Type double-spaced within and between entries in the MLA and APA styles. In the Chicago style, type single-spaced within each entry and double-spaced between entries.

A. The MLA Style

Preferred heading: Works Cited

BOOKS

One author

Seagrave, Sterling. The Marcos Dynasty. New York: Harper, 1988.

Two authors

Andrews, Deborah C., and William D. Andrews. Business Communication. New York: Macmillan, 1988.

Three authors

Allen, R. R., Kenneth L. Brown, and Joanne Yarvin. Learning Language through Communication: A Functional Perspective. Belmont, CA: Wadsworth, 1986.

More than three authors

Morris, Desmond, et al. Gestures. New York: Stein, 1979.

Editor

Johnson, Stanley, ed. The Population Problem. New York: Wiley, 1973.

Author and editor or translator

Fitzgerald, F. Scott. The Notebooks of F. Scott Fitzgerald. Ed. Matthew J. Bruccoli. New York: Harcourt, 1978.

Edition

Chenfield, Mimi Brodsky. Teaching Language Arts Creatively. 2nd ed. San Diego: Harcourt, 1987.

Book in several volumes

Fiedler, Leslie A. The Collected Essays of Leslie Fiedler. 2 vols. New York: Stein, 1971.

Essay or article in a collection	Agee, James. "Comedy's Greatest Era." <u>The Open Forum: Essays for Our Time</u>. Ed. Alfred Kazin. 3rd ed. New York: Harcourt, 1970. 339-357.
Bulletin or government publication	United States. Department of Agriculture. <u>The Face of Rural America: The Yearbook of Agriculture</u>. Washington: GPO, 1976. [GPO means Government Printing Office.]

ENCYCLOPEDIA ARTICLES

Signed or initialed (identified in key or guide)	Rupp, Ernest G. "Luther." <u>Encyclopaedia Britannica: Macropaedia.</u> 1988 ed.
Unsigned	"Binet, Alfred." <u>Encyclopedia Americana</u>. 1986 ed.

PERIODICAL ARTICLES

Magazine article (signed)	Tifft, Susan. "Who's Teaching Our Children?" <u>Time</u> 14 Nov. 1988: 58-64.
Magazine article (unsigned)	"Class Conflict." <u>Time</u> 14 Nov. 1988: 50.
Journal article (consecutive paging throughout volume)	Martin, Rita J. "Folk Songs as a Language Arts Experience." <u>Language Arts</u> 58 (1981): 326-329. [58 = vol. 58]
Journal article (new paging each issue)	Coleman, Eve B. "Flowcharting as a Prewriting Activity." <u>Computers, Reading, and Language Arts</u> 1.3 (1983): 36-38. [1.3 = vol. 1, no. 3]
Newspaper article (signed)	Lewis, Flora. "The Bad News Is Apathy." <u>New York Times</u> 9 Nov. 1988, late ed.: A35. [A35 = section A, p. 35]
Newspaper article or editorial (unsigned)	"In 1938, the World Knew." Editorial. <u>New York Times</u> 9 Nov. 1988, late ed.: A34.
Review	Drabelle, Dennis. "Marriage as Myth." Rev. of <u>Adultery: An Analysis of Love and Betrayal</u>, by Annette Lawson. <u>Psychology Today</u> Nov. 1988: 65.

UNPUBLISHED AND MISCELLANEOUS

Doctoral dissertation or master's thesis	Crips, Johanna. "The Impact of Television on Language Acquisition." Diss. Rutgers U, 1978.
Paper read or speech delivered but not published	Yesner, Seymour. "The Yellow Brick Road to Skills Land." NCTE Convention. San Diego, 29 Nov. 1975.
Interview	Ignatow, David. Personal interview. 26 Apr. 1989.

Nonprint medium	"Thinking." Narr. George Page. <u>The Mind</u>. Prod. and dir. Richard Hutton. PBS. WLIW, New York. 12 Dec. 1988. [TV program, part of series]
Computer software	<u>Interactive Authoring System</u>. Computer software. McGraw, 1983. IBM PC, 128KB, disk.

B. The APA Style*
Preferred heading: References

BOOKS

One author	Seagrave, S. (1988). <u>The Marcos dynasty</u>. New York: Harper & Row.
Two authors	Andrews, D. C., & Andrews, W. D. (1988). <u>Business communication</u>. New York: Macmillan.
Three authors	Allen, R. R., Brown, K. L., & Yatvin, J. (1986). <u>Learning language through communication: A functional perspective</u>. Belmont, CA: Wadsworth.
More than three authors	[Same form as for three authors. Give names of *all* authors.]
Editor	Johnson, S. (Ed.). (1973). <u>The population problem</u>. New York: Wiley.
Author and editor or translator	Freud, S. (1965). <u>The interpretation of dreams</u> (J. Strachey, Trans. and Ed.). New York: Avon Books. (Original work published 1900)
Edition	Chenfield, M. B. (1987). <u>Teaching language arts creatively</u> (2nd ed.). San Diego: Harcourt Brace Jovanovich.
Book in several volumes	Greenstein, F. I., & Polsby, N. W. (Eds.). (1984) <u>Handbook of political science</u> (Vol. 2). Reading, MA: Addison-Wesley.
Essay or article in a collection	Baker, L., & Brown, A. L. (1984). Metacognitive skills and reading. In P. D. Pearson (Ed.), <u>Handbook of reading research</u>. New York: Longman.
Bulletin or government publication	National Institute on Drug Abuse. (1979). <u>Research issues update, 1978</u> (NIDA Research Monograph No. 22). Washington, DC: U.S. Government Printing Office.

* This material is based on the *Publication Manual of the American Psychological Association* (3rd ed.). Copyright 1983 by the American Psychological Association. Publication by permission of the APA. Neither the original nor this adaptation can be republished, photocopied, reprinted, or distributed in any form, without the prior written permission of the APA.

ENCYCLOPEDIA ARTICLES

Signed or initialed (identified in key or guide)

George, B. J., Jr. (1983). Jurisdiction. In S. H. Kadish (Ed.), Encyclopedia of crime and justice (Vol. 3, pp. 922-926). New York: Free Press.

Unsigned

Barometric light. (1986). Encyclopedia Americana (Vol. 3, p. 258). Danbury, CT: Grolier.

PERIODICAL ARTICLES

Magazine article (signed)

Tifft, S. (1988, November 14). Who's teaching our children? Time, pp. 58-64.

Magazine article (unsigned)

Class conflict. (1988, November 14). Time, p. 50.

Journal article (consecutive paging throughout volume)

Weins, J. W. (1983). Metacognition and the adolescent learner. Journal of Learning Disabilities, 16, 144-149. [16 = vol. 16]

Journal article (new paging each issue)

Coleman, E. B. (1983). Flowcharting as a prewriting activity. Computers, Reading, and Language Arts, 1(3), 36-38. [1(3) = vol. 1, no. 3]

Newspaper article (signed)

Lewis, F. (1988, November 9). The bad news is apathy. New York Times, p. A35. [A35 = section A, p. 35]

Newspaper article or editorial (unsigned)

Swarm of "killer" bees found in Florida port. (1988, November 9). New York Times, p. A14.

Review

Drabelle, D. (1988). Marriage as myth. [Review of Adultery: An analysis of love and betrayal]. Psychology Today, 22(11), 65.

UNPUBLISHED OR MISCELLANEOUS

Doctoral dissertation or master's thesis

Bluedorn, A. C. (1976). A causal model of turnover in organizations. Dissertation Abstracts International, 37, 8004A. (University Microfilms No. 77-11, 730)

Paper read or speech delivered but not published

Schorr, F. (1982). Comprehending procedural instructions: The influence of metacognitive strategies. Paper presented at the meeting of the New England Educational Research Organization, Rockville, ME.

Interview

[Cite in text as a personal communication. Do not include in reference list.]

Nonprint medium

Molen, G. R. (Producer), & Levinson, B. (Director). (1988). Rain man [Film]. Hollywood, CA: United Artists.

Computer software	Roney, M. L., & O'Brien, T. C. (1985). <u>Planetary construction set: Discoveries in science</u> [Computer program]. Pleasantville, NY: Sunburst Communications.

C. The Chicago Style
Preferred heading: Bibliography

BOOKS

One author	Seagrave, Sterling. <u>The Marcos Dynasty</u>. New York: Harper & Row, 1988.
Two authors	Andrews, Deborah C., and William D. Andrews. <u>Business Communication</u>. New York: Macmillan, 1988.
Three authors	Allen, R. R., Kenneth L. Brown, and Joanne Yarvin. <u>Learning Language through Communication: A Functional Perspective</u>. Belmont, Ca.: Wadsworth, 1986.
More than three authors	[Same form as for three authors. Give names of all authors.]
Editor	Johnson, Stanley, ed. <u>The Population Problem</u>. New York: John Wiley and Sons, 1973.
Author and editor or translator	Fitzgerald, F. Scott. <u>The Notebooks of F. Scott Fitzgerald</u>. Edited by Matthew J. Bruccoli. New York: Harcourt Brace Jovanovich, 1978.
Edition	Chenfield, Mimi Brodsky. <u>Teaching Language Arts Creatively</u>. 2d ed. San Diego: Harcourt Brace Jovanovich, 1987.
Book in several volumes	Fielder, Leslie A. Vol. 1, <u>The Collected Essays of Leslie Fielder</u>. New York: Stein and Day, 1971.
Essay or article in a collection	Agee, James. "Comedy's Greatest Era." In <u>The Open Forum: Essays for Our Time</u>. 3d ed., ed. Alfred Kazin, 339-357. New York: Harcourt Brace Jovanovich, 1970.
Bulletin or government publication	U. S. Department of Agriculture. <u>The Face of Rural America: The Yearbook of Agriculture</u>. Washington: GPO, 1976. [GPO means Goverment Printing Office.]

ENCYCLOPEDIA ARTICLES

Signed or initialed (indentified in key or guide)	<u>Encyclopaedia Britannica: Macropaedia</u>. 1988 ed. S. v. "Luther, Martin" by Ernest G. Rupp. [S. v. means *sub voce*, "under the word."]
Unsigned	<u>Encyclopedia Americana</u>. 1986 ed. S. v. "Binet, Alfred."

PERIODICAL ARTICLES

Magazine article (signed)	Tifft, Susan. "Who's Teaching Our Children?" Time, 14 November 1988, 58-64.
Magazine article (unsigned)	"Class Conflict." Time, 14 November 1988, 50.
Journal article (consecutive paging throughout volume)	Martin, Rita J. "Folk Songs as a Language Arts Experience." Language Arts 58 (Fall 1981): 326-329. [58 = vol. 58]
Journal article (new paging each issue)	Coleman, Eve B. "Flowcharting as a Prewriting Activity." Computers, Reading, and Language Arts 1, no. 3 (1983): 36-38. [1 = vol. 1]
Newspaper article (signed)	Lewis, Flora. "The Bad News Is Apathy." New York Times, 9 November 1988, sec. A, p. 35.
Newspaper article or editorial (unsigned)	"In 1938, the World Knew." New York Times 9 November 1988, sec. A, p. 34.
Review	Drabelle, Dennis. "Marriage as Myth." Review of Adultery: An Analysis of Love and Betrayal, by Annette Lawson. Psychology Today, November 1988, 65.

UNPUBLISHED AND MISCELLANEOUS

Doctoral dissertation or master's thesis	Crips, Johanna. "The Impact of Television on Language Acquisition." Ph.D. diss., Rutgers University, 1978.
Paper read or speech delivered but not published	Yesner, Seymour. "The Yellow Brick Road to Skills Land." Paper presented at the annual NCTE Convention, San Diego, November 1975.
Interview	Ivers, David. Interview by Joseph Higgins. Boston, Massachusetts, 26 April 1991.
Nonprint medium	"Thinking." The Mind. Prod. and dir. Richard Hutton. PBS. WLIW, New York. 12 December 1988. [TV program, part of series. NOTE: The Chicago style requires only that enough information be given to enable others to find the material.]
Computer Software	Interactive Authoring System. New York: McGraw-Hill, 1983.

INDEX